Writing Exposition

A Program For Expository Writing

a
publication
of

NATIONAL WRITING INSTITUTE
624 W. University #248
Denton, TX 76201-1889

ISBN 1-888344-02-4

Manufactured in the United States of America

For information, write: National Writing Institute
                           624 W. University #248
                           Denton, TX 76201-1889

                           call: 1 (800) 688-5375
                           e-mail: info@writingstrands.com

NATIONAL WRITING INSTITUTE PUBLICATIONS
and
SERVICE

STUDENTS
Writing Strands Level 1
Writing Strands Level 2
Writing Strands Level 3
Writing Strands Level 4
Writing Strands Level 5
Writing Strands Level 6
Writing Strands Level 7
Writing Exposition
Creating Fiction

Communication And Interpersonal Relationships
Dragonslaying Is For Dreamers
Axel Meets The Blue Men
Axel's Challenge

PARENTS/TEACHERS

Evaluating Writing
Reading Strands

Analyzing The Novel:
Dragonslaying Is For Dreamers

This book is dedicated to the wonderful young minds that taught me to teach.

Dear Fellow Writer,

Congratulations. You've come a long way, whether it was with the *Writing Strands* program or some other one, you're now ready to learn to write the academic papers colleges require. The exercises in this book aren't easy, and that's good, for if you work hard on them with a strong desire to use your language with precision, you'll be able to handle any writing assignment you'll be given throughout college.

If you haven't used Writing Strands materials before and you have a year or so to get ready for college work, you should start with Writing Strands Levels 4 or 5. If you don't do this catch-up work, you might find that this book is too much of a challenge. You would be able to write the assignments, but you might not benefit from them as much as you should.

When you think you're finished with each assignment, check back over the directions and make sure you've completed correctly every part. Then read the student paper in the appendix that was generated by the same assignment. This will let you know if you're working hard enough. Don't be discouraged if you don't think your papers are as good as the examples in this book, for they were written over many times. You may have to work that hard to do as well.

When you're done and you're satisfied with your work, you'll find that all the effort's been worth it. Soon, when you have to write college papers or when your boss asks you to write reports, you'll be very glad you worked so hard.

Good luck and don't expect to be perfect. None of us is.

Sincerely,

Dave Marks

CONTENTS   page

NOT RULES,
BUT
THINGS TO THINK ABOUT

In almost everything we do, there are rules (like laws), and then there are what we call "rules." The rules that are like laws are written, and we all accept these as the rules we have to live by. Then there are the "rules," the things that we *should* do, that we agree to do, and things that make life nicer if we do them.

This is also true in writing. As an example of the difference in the rules of writing, look at the rule (law) that says that every sentence must start with a capital letter. This is written down and we all must write using this rule. A "rule" of writing is that we use an exclamation point only once a year.

The following "rules" are just strong suggestions. You can violate them if you want to. It might be good to keep in mind however, that if you do, your college teachers or bosses will look at your writing the same way that company at dinner might look at you if you burped at the end of the meal. So, below is a short list of the "rules" of writing:

1. Don't use exclamation points! This makes any writing look amateurish and fuzzy. If you're saying something that's important, the way you say it should be strong enough so that you don't have to tell your reader that it's important by using exclamation points at the end of your sentences.

2. Don't underline the titles of your papers. The only time there should be an underline in one of your titles is when you use the names of books or magazines in the title.

3. Skip a line after the title in any paper you're giving to someone else to read.

4. Never put "The End" at the end of anything you write for school.

5. Don't try writing humor until you've studied it and really know the difference between being funny and being corny. (Those places in this book where I've tried to be funny and was just corny will give you an example of what I mean.)

6. Don't skip a line between paragraphs.

7. Always leave a margin at the bottom of each page.

8. Check your papers for clichés before you write the final drafts.

LIBRARY MANUAL

This exercise has been designed to help you learn to:
1. Use all the facilities in a library
2. Arrange a mass of information into a usable form
3. Explain how to use a library

Many public libraries have manuals which are given to interested members. Very often they're the result of a group effort over many years and reflect the desires of a number of people who wish to include things and to write what they think would reflect well on themselves or on the library.

A well written manual is a tool. It makes no sense to have flowers painted on a wrench, just as it makes no sense to have them on a manual of operation. The user of a manual wants information, and that's all. Any words that are unnecessary for the conveying of that information just get in the way of the manual's use.

In this exercise you'll write a manual for a library. It will help you to do a good job if you keep in mind how a reader might use it.

Usually, the reader of a manual wants only one piece of information. This means that the manual should be written in such a way that that one piece of information is all the user has to read. The reader should be able to open the manual to the table of contents, find the listing for what is wanted, turn to the indicated page and read the desired information. Anything else the user has to read should not be there.

Paragraphs should not be used when a sentence would do. Sentences should not be used when a single word would do. Procedures should be listed and numbered. There should be headings for each entry, and these should be outdented or underlined so that they can be seen easily.

There's no problem with multiple entries in the manual. In fact, this should be the case. Since the user usually will want only one piece of information, the repetition of information will not be offensive.

Under the section where the user is instructed in the procedure for checking out a fiction book, there might be a listing for a fine in case the book were to be returned late. In the section where the user is instructed in the procedure for taking out a nonfiction book, the same information about the book being overdue should appear or the user should be referred to the page where that information could be found. In this section of your manual you should list the steps the user must take to check out a book. These should be numbered in the order they should be taken.

Most users of libraries are familiar with the card catalogue, but are not sure how to use all of the information contained on each card. The inclusion of this information in your manual would make it a more valuable instrument. Your library might have a computer for the selection of books from the catalogue. If this is the case, by all means explain its use and give examples. The student paper in the appendix of this book does not have that explained because the library used did not have that facility, but many university libraries do.

The easiest way for a user of your manual to receive this information is for you to reproduce a card from the catalogue and to draw an arrow from each entry to some explanation in the margin of the page. In this way the user need look at only the one piece of information to get the desired help. This same procedure should apply to the section on "The Guide to Periodical Literature." You should have an example entry and show with arrows and explanations what information each part of the entry gives the reader. You may find it convenient to do the same thing in the part where you explain how to check out a book or magazine. There should be a floor plan of the rooms in your library so the user can find what is needed. In the section on reference books, it might be a good idea to refer the reader to the floor plan.

A good way to determine if a piece of information or any section should be in your manual would be to ask yourself this question: "Would a reader need to know this, and if so, is this the briefest way it can be put?" If you do this you won't be inclined to include a section on the library's history or to have an introduction.

A good manual should have an extensive table of contents that contains a listing for every bit or category of information the user could want. This should be ordered alphabetically so the user can find quickly that one piece of information needed. The page numbers in the table of contents will not be in order, but that makes no difference at all.

It would not be possible for you to list all of the kinds of books in your library. You might include a chart showing the Dewey system of classification. In the section on reference books, you'll not be able to list all of the kinds of materials available, but you should be able to list groups of materials. For instance, you could list literary references, and direct the user to that section on the shelves.

When you make your floor plan, of course you would not include the tables and chairs, but you might indicate where the major sources of information are located, like the map cabinet. I would suggest you start this exercise by making the floor plan and then mark on it the location of all of the materials. Before you start your paper read the student paper in the appendix.

LIBRARY MANUAL NOTES

One of the major problems in this exercise is organization. It might help you to list all of the items, services and resources you can find in your library. The following list might help you.

1. Fiction:

2. Periodicals and Newspapers:

3. Audio-Visual:

4. Non-Fiction:

5. Reference:

6. Procedures:

A Good way to find out what a user of your manual might need to know is to think through a typical assignment. Pick any subject and write down just how a student would find all the information and use all of the services. If the student had to do a report on some aspect of the American Civil War, list how that student would find information and use and/or check it out. Below is a listing of some of the major areas you should think about for this assignment:

Maps:

Biographies of military leaders:

Fictional accounts:

Film strips:

Magazine articles:

Newspaper clippings:

History books:

Records:

Paintings and photographs:

FAIR

This argumentative essay exercise was designed to help you learn to:
1. Use models to aid you in understanding the present and in anticipating future events
2. Use hypothetical situations as support in exposition
3. Understand the nature and function of abstractions as they guide your life
4. Use logic and knowledge to resist the acceptance of jingoism

Most young people of high school age, being fairly naive, tend to accept the values that they're given by any adult source—even if they come to them through television—not questioning either the source or the implications inherent in their acceptance. One of the benefits of this exercise is that you'll have a chance to look objectively at a word that is very familiar to you, one which you think you understand and believe is good for you. This exercise is not given as a way for you to question the values given to you by your parents or your church. Those are given to you with your best interests at heart. But all of your life you'll be asked to believe things and accept the ideas represented by words and\or abstract concepts that will not be given to you for your benefit but to aid those people giving you the ideas.

For example, think of the words that describe the value of diamonds. Many of us believe that diamonds are rare and very valuable. We have been told that they last forever. Jewelry store owners and the owners of diamond companies advertise precious stones, and in these advertisements you're told how valuable diamonds are. This information is not given to you to help you in any way. In truth, diamonds are a controlled commodity and the value, or price, is fixed by a cartel run by the De Beers Company. Gem quality stones have no intrinsic value, and their distribution is so tightly managed, to keep the price up, that this company has had to spend hundreds of millions of dollars to buy the production of Russian and Australian diamond mines. The "value" of a diamond is not a real thing, but is a manufactured idea of value.

In this paper you're to demonstrate that it's easy for people to misunderstand some of the abstractions which are used to dictate beliefs and actions. To do this you'll take one such abstraction, examine it, and show what it really means. You might find this exercise unsettling; if you find a word that right now means so much to you, and in writing this essay, you discover that it doesn't really mean what you thought it did, then you'll begin to ask yourself the question: Do I really want to be guided by my previous understanding of this word? Some examples of such words might include, *responsibility, justice, freedom, truth,* and the one you're going to work with, *fair*.

It's very common to hear children cry out on the playground and even sometimes at home, "That's not fair!" What is really meant is that they do not like it, it's hard, or it's inconvenient. They have a clearly defined concept of fair that has nothing at all to do with the word as it's understood and used in the educated, adult world.

1. You should begin this exercise with an explanation of *abstractions*. You might use the notes page at the end of this exercise to do this.
2. Make a list of some of the abstractions and their definitions which people use to help them make decisions. You'll find that some of the words which they or even you might use to make decisions are not as clearly understood as you thought they were.
3. You should include a definition of *fair* in the list for point #2. It would be good if you were to ask some others what they think *fair* means. You might get definitions like, "Equal distribution, Equality, Even-handedness," and, "Everybody getting the same amount."

The information you put in the backgrounds of your papers is intended to give your readers that information which will allow them to understand your contentions. In this paper, your readers have to know that there have been a number of political and cultural influences which have given the American middle class its concept of what is fair, and this group of people has passed this concept on to its children. Some of these influences have been:

A. The "Magna Carta" which gave us the idea that power should not be only in the hands of one man but that it should be shared;

B. "The Declaration of Independence" which gives us the idea that people should be treated equally;

C. The "Constitution of the United States" which denies special treatment to any person or group;

D. Organized sports which have given us the idea that we must all follow the same rules, and that there must be an evenness of forces in confrontation, (the same number of players of similar skill for each side);

E. Our religious backgrounds which have given us the idea that there's value in equal treatment and that justice is possible;

F. Our educational systems which tell us that all people should have equal opportunities;

G. Our judicial system which is based on the concept that all people will be treated equally under the law.

4. You should use this idea in your paper, even beginning with these same words: "If there were some way to impose these concepts of fairness on the entire world, my life would be changed greatly for the better/worse (you have a choice here) in terms of. . ." You might choose to include such areas as: educational opportunities, life expectancy, anticipated life income, health and diet.

5. An example of how much your life might be changed if the agreed upon concept of fair were to be imposed on the whole world would be clear if you were to look at your educational opportunities.

   If all the education in the world were to be equally divided among all the world's people, the opportunity for schooling for everyone would not go beyond the fourth grade level. This would have tremendous implications for your reader, because, if no one could have an education past the fourth grade, there would no doctors, scientists, engineers, or any professional people at all. There would be no new technology and no one to repair what technology we now have. You and your reader would have to live in a rural and primitive agrarian society. You would not have your own phone, bedroom, car, future schooling, clothes or most of the things you see as making your life fun, and what some people call "the good life" would end.

   You'll have to make clear to your reader that the change to a fair world would mean that there could be no new opportunities or objects produced so as to make more opportunities, but that those things which now exist would have to be evenly divided. The world's people would have to share equally what is now available. The same condition would hold true for food, telephones, refrigerators, cars, health and all the other conditions of life.

6. A model is a small, easily handled and studied copy of a large object or idea. Models are created because of cost and convenience. A model of anything is like a child's toy plane. The toy is something the child can handle and control. It's used to teach the child what a real plane is like but is in a form the child can relate to. Models can be created to allow people to study cities, institutions, concepts, future situations, and in our case, an abstraction and its implications.

7. In this paper you'll be using the future perfect tense. You should begin the hypothetical situation in the introduction with the word *if*: "If a way were to be found to impose on the whole world this concept of *fair*, my life would change. . ." or, "I would have less . . ." or, "People would not be. . ." or, "There would be no. . ." or, ". . .cars would be divided among. . . ."

8. The process statement for this paper will consist of the way you indicate your life would change:"My life would change for the worse in terms of my life expectancy, my educational opportunities and the kinds and amounts of food I would be able to eat."

INTRODUCTION

Your introduction should contain:

1. The idea that abstractions are very important in guiding people's lives
2. A short explanation of where most Americans get their ideas of what is fair
3. The idea that it's important that people understand not only what abstractions mean but also accept what the implications are of using the abstractions to help them make decisions
4. The hypothetical situation about making the whole world fair
5. The process which will contain the list of what in your life would change if the world were to be reorganized according to the American concept of "fair."

BODY

The body of this paper will have two parts, as indicated by the process, which should start like this: 1) "My life would change. . .in terms of. . ." This means you'll have to explain what your life is like now in those respects, and 2) what your life would be like if the world were to be changed so that the generally accepted meaning of the word *fair* were able to be imposed upon it.

Example:

If you were to decide to use food as one process point, you would have to explain what kinds and what amounts of food you have now and then what kinds and what amounts would be available after the change to a fair world. The first half of the body would have to explain about the refrigerator and cupboards at home being full of food and that you can go to them at any time and eat. Also, that you have access to any number of restaurants and usually have money to buy food when you are hungry, and that you have well balanced meals and consume on average two thousand to three thousand calories a day. The second part of the body would have to contain an explanation of the food situation in the rest of the world now where one third of all the people go to bed hungry every night, and one fifth of the people are starving.

If all the food in the world were to be evenly divided among the world's people, you might receive only one thousand calories a day and you would not have the variety you now enjoy. Of course, this would have to have an effect on your health and life expectancy.

Once you've chosen those areas of life you're going to examine, you should go to the library and do the research necessary to understand the situation in other areas of the world. Encyclopedias, almanacs, and magazine articles should give you the information you need.

CONCLUSION

1. There should be some connection made between the observations you made in the introduction about the importance of abstractions and the implications of your accepting them.
2. There should be a statement near the end of the conclusion about your new understanding of what it would be like if things were to be fair.
3. There should be a statement at the end of the conclusion about your awareness of the necessity of careful thought when given abstractions and told to guide your life by them.

FAIR NOTES

1. Definition of *Abstraction*:

_____

_____

_____

2. List of abstract concept that help you make decisions:

_____   _____

_____   _____

_____   _____

3. Your definition of *fair*:

_____

_____

_____

4. The conclusion you've come to about abstractions:

_____

_____

5. Your **contention** based on that conclusion:

_____

_____

_____

6. Your **process** sentence which will explain how you'll support that contention:

_____

_____

_____

BOOK COVERS

This argumentative exercise was designed to help you learn:
1. The structure of an argumentative paper
2. To use your own experience in support of an argument
3. The parts of a paperback book cover that indicate its type and reading level

It's a problem to know, when in a bookstore amid hundreds of available selections, which book might be a good selection. Without a system to help make the choice, a person is restricted to making the decision on the basis of whether or not the cover looks exciting.

Fortunately, it's not true that you cannot tell a book by its cover. If we consider the cover to include the covering material and the first few pages of a paperback book, we can tell a great deal about it. In this argumentative paper, you'll demonstrate that the old saying about telling a book by its cover is not true.

There's a relationship between the sophistication of the art on a paperback book cover and the sophistication of the writing in the book. Generally speaking, the more sophisticated the art, the better the writing.

In many paperback books, the publishers list suggested further readings, indicating that if you liked this book you might like these others. You might be familiar with some of the titles. If so, it would give you some idea of the level of reading of the book in question.

Many paperback books have review blurbs on the covers or on the first few pages. If this is not the case, the book is either a literary classic which needs no reviewer's comments, or it's so poorly written it has not been reviewed.

Even the reviewers will give you information. If the major large city newspapers or nationally known reviewers have reviewed the book, it very well might be a better choice than if the reviewers were from small town papers.

The copyright date and the number of printings will give you an indication of the popularity of the book. If the book is in its third or fourth printing, you'll know it has been popular.

The picture on the cover of a paperback can give you strong indications of the type of book it is. Some of the genres are obviously related to the pictures. Gothic mysteries almost always have a young lady in a long dress running from a large house. The art is usually romantic. Historical romances have a man and a woman in period dress. Westerns have men in western clothes, usually with horses. Novels which have swastikas on the covers deal with the threat of, the history of, or the rebirth of the Nazi movement. Young girl romances have pictures with soft lines, pastel colors, pictures showing young girls, and in the background there are often boys of the same age. There are many other types of covers which you'll discover.

The best way for you to do this exercise is to go to the library and take a large pile of paperback books and line them up on one of the tables. Group them in categories of reading by the above method. You'll quickly begin to see patterns.

You're to write a persuasive paper with the position that you *can* tell a book by its cover.

CULTURAL STABILITY

This argumentative exercise was designed to help you learn that:
1. Cultural values are important and are transmitted from generation to generation
2. The influences children are subjected to shape their values
3. You must come to some conclusion for yourself about the benefits of our cultural values
4. You can integrate these ideas and conclusions into a paper that presents how you feel about contemporary culture

We place our values, known by the labels of "good" and "bad," on beliefs, objects and institutions. If we believe that good health is important, we have health as a value. This would help us make many of the decisions about our activities. It would mean that we would decide to exercise and eat healthy foods, to have regular medical checkups and not to smoke or use drugs.

Most people are under the impression that the values they hold are ones that they decided upon for themselves. This paper is designed to examine the ways that many of the young people in this country have adopted their values. Every day we see the results of young people adopting destructive values—gang shootings, crack houses, runaways, violence in schools, and the great increase in alcohol use. This paper is in no way intended to have you evaluate your value choices, or to encourage you to change your values. Those are yours. It's intended to encourage you to examine the ways many middle class American young people get the values they hold.

Just as individual values determine what each of us does, the values of a culture determine group activities. If each generation in any culture were to create for itself new values, there would be no continuity in our culture from one generation to the next. You can see the chaos that would ensue if one generation were to decide that zoos were a good way to show children what animals are like and spent a great deal of money building zoos and stocking them with wild animals from all over the world, and the next generation were to decide that zoos are cruel places and had the animals sent back to their natural homes and had the zoos torn down. This example makes it easy to see the necessity of stabilizing cultural values by having each generation pass the values it holds on to its children.

To this end, every culture has developed what are called cultural perpetuators. These are institutions and practices that teach the young people of the culture the values currently held by the adults. All cultures have developed means of educating their young. Usually, the more developed the culture, the more sophisticated are the educational institutions. In America, we have developed an extensive educational system, and many of the wonderful things you see young people doing on television they learned in school.

Still, in our culture, parents are the major influencers of children. They pass on their values to their children by making decisions about their participation in various activities. Fathers teach their sons values when they select toys for them. If a father were to give his son a football or a gun, he would transmit different values than he would if he were to give him a microscope and a set of science books.

Social scientists tell us that not much reliability can be placed on what people say their values are, rather, individual or group values can be determined only by an examination of the time, money and energy spent on objects and activities. For example, if a boy spends most of his time and money working on and fixing up his car, and only a few minutes a day with his girlfriend, he couldn't get away with saying that he values his girl more than he does his car. In the same way, in many cases, this selection of time, money and energy by parents transmits a value message to their children.

Other than direct parental influences, some of the major transmitters of values in our culture are:
1. Churches
2. Toys
3. Clothes
4. Games
5. Schools
6. Books
7. Leisure time activities
8. Television
9. Organizations like Cub Scouts and 4-H Clubs

In this exercise you'll pick one or two values you feel are representative of the majority of American middle class values and demonstrate to your reader how these values are given to children.

You'll have to decide for yourself what the values in our culture are and how they're transmitted. For example, if you were to decide that America is a sexist country because girls are discriminated against, you would have to show your reader how this sexism is transmitted from one generation to the next.

You might be able to find and give examples from children's books that show the wife in the kitchen fixing dinner when the father comes home from "work." You might be able to find catalogues from stores that have dress-up outfits, showing pictures of airline pilot outfits for boys and stewardess outfits for girls, football outfits for boys and cheerleader outfits for girls, and doctor outfits for boys and nurse outfits for girls. In the toy sections you might be able to find construction toys for boys and tiny stoves and dishwashers for girls. If you were to find this condition in a catalogue, you would have to decide whether this was an indication of a cultural value and whether this might be a method by which parents could pass this value on to their children.

Keep in mind that the store which sells toys does not choose which toys to sell based on the values of the store owner. The demand for the toys is the basis on which the selection by the store owner is made. This demand is created mainly by television advertising. The children tell their parents what they want, and then the parents have to decide for themselves what they want their children to have. It's the parents who decide what values to transmit to their children.

You might take the following steps in the writing of this paper:
1. Decide on the major values of our culture.
2. Select one or two to use as examples.
3. List the perpetuators you feel transmit the value or values.
4. Decide how you feel about this situation—this will produce your contention.
5. Use your list of perpetuators as key words in your process.
6. Write the background using an intelligent adult as your audience.
7. Have examples for every position you take in the paper.

If you talk about children's books, you should name the books and include quotations in support of your points. If you use catalogues, you should cut out pictures and put them in your paper. If you use songs that children sing in clubs, or if you use TV shows, or games that children play, use examples directly from them. If you use church activities, you should give examples from church situations.

NOTES ON PERPETUATORS

What you see as the main middle class values in our culture:
1. _____
2. _____
3. _____
4. _____
5. _____
6. _____
The one or two you plan to use as examples and the methods of transmitting them:

1. _____
   Transmitters:_____
2. _____
   Transmitters: _____

Introduction:

1. How you feel about American values and the methods of perpetuating them:

   _____
   _____
   _____

2. This conclusion about how you feel stated as a contention:

   _____
   _____
   _____

3. Your perpetuators listed as key words for your process:

1) _____ 4) _____
2) _____ 5) _____
3) _____ 6) _____

4. Your process sentence:

_____
_____
_____

Conclusion:

1. Write your contending idea in a different form for the conclusion:

_____
_____

2. Make the connection between the body, contention and background:

_____
_____

3. Since this as an argumentative exposition, you must use the fourth conclusion step—the asking of the reader to accept your position:

_____
_____
_____

ROLE MODELS

This argumentative exercise was designed to help you learn to:
1. Recognize the function of one step in the process of child development in our society
2. Compare an ideal situation with an actual one
3. Predict the consequences of a decision
4. Structure an argumentative paper based on this experience
5. Present your views convincingly

The people who study how children develop their personalities tell us that each child "tries on" a number of "characters" before the child settles on one that is suitable. This is most evident when children are very young. We see them in Superman or nurse outfits. When they're older we see them adopt the dress and styles of movie and television stars. Young teens often adopt the manners of their peers whom they respect.

The types of heroes children have has changed since the advent of television. Many children now have as heroes people who play the roles of anti-heroes. These are characters who fight against enemies the children can understand are bad, but the characters do so in ways that might not be traditional or "good."

The children who identify with anti-heroes may adopt some of the characteristics which create the "anti" part of their characters.

An example of how this may work is seen in the re-runs of the television show, *Mash*. Hawkeye Pierce is an anti-hero. He relentlessly chases nurses, drinks to excess, is disrespectful to his superiors, and makes his own illegal alcohol. If a young boy were to identify with Hawkeye, he might adopt both his hero and his anti-hero characteristics. And in this adoption lies a possible problem.

Many years ago a very popular program for children was *The Dukes of Hazard*. The Duke brothers are anti-heroes who perform in very anti-social ways. They have no jobs, they're just out of jail for running moonshine, they have invested all of their money in a car which they drive very fast right through town, they have no respect for the law and break it constantly, they're the cause of the sheriff repeatedly crashing his police car and they have no ambition to accept the responsibilities of adult life. Even though they are heroes in the show, if young people were to use them as role models, as I'm sure some do, the young people could copy patterns of behavior and methods of solving problems that could be very anti-social.

19

In this exercise you do not need to support the idea that children watching television will be damaged by it. You may decide that children now, because of television, have a great choice of heroes from which to chose their role models, many being very admirable. There are many people on news, sports, religious and talk shows who could become positive role models for young people. You'll have to decide the position you adopt.

You're to examine models you find available for children to copy from either TV or the movies and come to some conclusion about them, and then you're to turn that conclusion into a **contention** for this paper.

Your **background** will be an introduction to the creation and function of role models for children.

Your **process** for this paper will be a listing of your examples of role models and the kinds of behaviors they promote.

The **body** will contain the examples of the listing in the process. Since this is an argumentative exposition, there will be four points you're to make in the **conclusion**.

ROLE MODEL NOTES

1. The two or three characters you'll use as examples:

    A._____

    B._____

    C._____

2. The characteristics of these characters:

    A. 1) _____   3) _____
          2) _____   4) _____

    B. 1) _____   3) _____
          2) _____   4) _____

    C. 1) _____   3) _____
          2) _____   4) _____

The results of children adopting these characters as role models:

Character A. _____

_____

_____

Character B. _____

_____

_____

Character C. _____

_____

_____

The conclusion you've come to because of this understanding:

_____

_____

_____

The contention you developed from that conclusion:

_____

_____

_____

The key words for your process statement:

_____   _____

_____   _____

_____   _____

The words to the final step in the conclusion to this argumentative exposition:

_____

_____

_____

_____

_____

COMPARISON AND CONTRAST
IN
DISCRIMINATION

This explanatory exercise was designed to help you:
1. Recognize the similarities and differences in two similar but slightly different objects
2. Organize these similarities and differences into categories
3. Come to come conclusions about this process that can be used to construct a contention for an explanatory exposition on discrimination
4. Write a paper about the process of discrimination in which you'll discriminate between two objects which you'll describe in detail in an objective way

One part of this exercise is similar to one that is very often given in colleges to students in their freshmen year. The assignment directions most often will be brief: "I want you to write a 1,000 word paper comparing two objects or conditions. Use detail in description, and make sure you write in complete paragraphs." Sometimes the directions will include the understanding that comparison includes both similarities and differences. But very seldom will the students be given any direction about how to structure their examination of the objects or the structure of their papers. The following exercise can be a useful guide.

You'll write an explanatory exposition of at least 800 words about the process of discrimination, and in doing so you'll examine two similar but slightly different objects. This will give you experience in recognizing details and in recording what you observe.

You may choose any two objects you wish, but you should keep in mind that the more complicated the objects are the more complicated will be the differences.

This paper should demonstrate to your reader that to discriminate wisely means that care has to be taken in examining the objects or options available. This idea should be supported by and limited to an examination of the two objects. The background should suggest that the process of discrimination is important if people are to make good decisions.

The **background** for this paper should introduce to your reader the consequences of the lack of care in decision making; what faulty discrimination has cost us as a country or as a group of people. Your reader should be told that this process is extremely complicated, and to demonstrate this complexity, you're going to compare and contrast two similar but different objects that are very simple. This will show your reader how complicated the process of discrimination is for complicated decisions. This will help you to convince your reader of the importance of this process you're going to demonstrate.

The **process** sentence should tell your reader that you're creating an example of the process of examination using the two objects and mention the areas of similarity and difference you plan to examine. Of course, the process will depend on the objects, but there are some general rules that should apply. Some areas that might fit most objects are: weight, size, durability, cost, materials made from, color, function, flexibility, resistance to heat/cold/pressure, and repairability. In this background, it might be helpful to your reader if you were to talk about the importance of making a careful examination of the choices available in any situation where decisions have to be made.

The **body** can be set up by showing the similarities first then the differences for each area of examination, or by showing the similarities and differences simultaneously for each area.

THE USE OF *I*

This exercise was designed to help you learn to:
1. Engineer experiences in support of an hypothesis
2. Transcribe conversations
3. Use primary resources as supportive material for a paper
4. Appreciate the effect of the use of personal pronouns on conversation patterns

One common characteristic of the conversations of young people is that they have not yet learned to disguise the selfish nature of their interests. Almost all teenage conversational responses begin with the use of the word *I*. This does not make the speakers poor at conversation, just not as sophisticated at hiding their self-interest as are people of more experience. Your experience with this condition will be the basis of this explanatory paper.

This exercise will have three parts:

1. The **first part** will be your engineering of **three conversations** in which you'll vary the frequency of your use of the word *I* and the taking of notes of your conversational partners' reactions.

2. The **second part** will be your **transcription** of the conversations and an analysis of them. This is where you'll record the effect on your conversational partners of your changing of the frequency of your use of *I*.

3. The **third part** will be the **writing of an expository paper** explaining what effect the use of the first person pronoun has on a listener. You'll use your experiences in the three conversations as support in the body of this paper.

PART ONE:

You're to set up conversations with three acquaintances who are not your good friends. Of course, you're not to discuss doing this paper with them.

In the **first** conversation, you'll use *I* a great deal, and you'll talk about things in which only you have an interest.

In the second conversation, you'll use both *I* and *you* and talk about things that are of interest

25

to both you and the other person.

In the **third** conversation, you're not to use *I* at all. You'll find this hard to do, and you may have to have a number of conversations before you have one where you're successful. In this conversation you'll talk only about things of interest to the other person.

PART TWO:

You'll transcribe (write) the three conversations and make notes about the frequency and kind of reinforcements (encouragements to keep talking) in each one. This should be done as soon as the conversations end; you'll be surprised at how well you remember what was said. You should record the reinforcements at the same time you transcribe the conversations. When what is said is reinforced by a listener, the listener nods, says "uh huh," smiles, laughs or gives some other like response.

You should also record negative reinforcements, such as when the listener looks away from you, plays with an object in front of him, looks around the room or shuffles his feet or makes similar impatient gestures.

PART THREE:

You're to write an explanatory exposition based on the experiences you had in the three conversations and supporting a contention based on a conclusion you've come to from the experience. For each of the experiences of support for the body, you should introduce your reader to the conversation by a description of its location, the people involved, and the techniques used.

USE OF *I* NOTES

1. The conclusion you've come to from the three conversations:

_____
_____
_____

2. The contention you've developed from this conclusion:

_____
_____

3. The key words you'll use in the process:

A_____ B _____C _____

4. The process sentence containing the key words:

_____

_____

_____

5. The ideas you must use in the background to introduce your contention to your reader:

A. _____

   _____

   _____

B. _____

   _____

   _____

C. _____

   _____

   _____

REACTION PAPER

One of the activities that is most characteristic of the education process is that of teachers exposing their students to ideas and information and having them react to them. The classes you'll have that will have the most influence on you and you will think will have been of the most benefit will be those which will have been centered on student activity. We learn the most when we act and react. Good teachers will understand and practice this. In their classes you often will be asked to react in writing. This will be in the form of essay tests, themes and what are called papers. The papers will often be reactions to something you've been given to read: articles, essays, theories, papers in professional journals, books or monographs. What your teachers will want will be your reaction to the ideas. They won't expect you to agree with or to like the writers' efforts, but they'll always expect you to respond to the writing in an organized way.

LENGTH

As a general rule, the longer the writing you're reacting to the longer should be your reaction. If you're reacting to a book you might figure on producing five or six pages. If you're reacting to an article in a magazine plan on two to three pages. Of course, there's no point in ever writing more than you need to to get your point across. Other than finding out if you've read the article, your instructors will want to know how you feel about your exposure to the ideas in the writing, and they'll want to find these things out without reading any more than they have to. Unless otherwise indicated, such as your instructor saying, "Just keep notes on file cards on the articles you've read," a minimum length for your paper will be about two pages.

STRUCTURE

Often your instructor will give you length and content guidelines to follow. In this case by all means follow the suggestions. If you're not given a guide, this outline should work.

1. It would be good to **comment** on either the **author or the piece** in the opening sentence. "B.F. Skinner has again ignored all the latest research in psychology in his latest piece in the June issue of *Psychology*."

2. State the author's **main and subordinate ideas**. These should be labeled as such: "The main thrust of Skinner's article is his reaffirmation of his earlier claims that people can be programmed. He supports this idea by again referring to his work with birds, and he even

reintroduces the reader to the success he had with the conditioning of his daughter."

3. **Agree with or refute** all or parts of the work.

You should let the teacher know how you feel about what you've read. In this you should, as for most of your courses, refer to other experts in the field. Unless told otherwise, you should not assume the position of expert in your reaction papers. In your acceptance or rejection of the author's ideas, give other expert views as justification for your decisions: *"Skinner's refusal to give up his "birds" is hard to understand in light of research done in the past six years in the field of animal and human psychology. In 1989 Barnhardt and Stimson at U.C.L.A. found that animal behavioral motivation was in no way analogous to human behavior. In 1984 Cruthburg at the University of Michigan established that operant conditioning as practiced with animals had no correlation with expected results with the same practices when applied to human behavior."*

4. Come to some **conclusion about the value** of the piece for your field. *"This article is extremely important, for it should put to rest once and for all the questions people have about the seeding of this planet from outer space as a genesis factor."*

5. State how you feel about how **well the author achieved** the stated or implied intent. *"If the general's intent was to discredit all TV journalism he did a credible job."*

To give you some experience in this type of academic writing, you should read an article (this means non-fiction) in a recent (this means in the last six months) non-technical magazine (this means one published for the non-professional in the field) and using these suggestions and write a reaction paper to it.

REACTION NOTES

1. The article studied for this exercise: _____

   Author: _____
2. The main point of the article:

   _____
   _____
   _____

3. The support points:

A. _____
B. _____
C. _____
D. _____

4. The points you agree with and why:

A. _____
B. _____
C. _____
D. _____

5. The points you disagree with and why:

A. _____
B. _____
C. _____
D. _____

BIASING

There are three papers in this exercise:
1. A biased ten-question survey
2. An exposition (argumentative) of about 1200 words
3. An exposition (explanatory) of about 1000 to 1,400 words

PAPER ONE (SURVEY) was designed to help you learn:

1. How to select survey respondents by cross-sectioning a population
2. How to write biased and bias-free survey questions
3. How to collate survey responses to demonstrate a point

PAPER TWO (ARGUMENT) was designed to help you learn:

1. How to recognize a writer's unfair attempt to influence a reader by doing it yourself
2. How to hide your biasing attempts in an ostensibly objective paper
3. How to structure effective arguments

PAPER THREE (EXPLANATION) was designed to help you learn:

1. How to come to a conclusion from your own experiences
2. How to use primary research to support your papers

This three-part exercise was designed to teach you enough about biasing in writing so that you might appreciate the use of words in precise ways, and also so that you might be able to protect yourself when others try to influence you unfairly.

PAPER #1

The first paper is to be the results of an opinion survey. This will not be an essay, but will just be your results. This can be in the form of a report of the ability you developed in influencing your respondents. You can format this report in any way that you care to. It does not have to be formal.

You're to orally survey 30 people on their opinions on one or more current issues. The respondents are to be a cross-section of some group. They might be chosen from your youth group, church membership, 4H Club, Scout Troop, choir or any other group you might have access to. This group can be divided by sex, age, grade, race, belief or any other method. A cross section of any group will show a representative portion of each section of the whole population in the entire group. If half of your respondents are male, then those 15 people would represent the male population of the whole group. That whole group could be the population of your town, church, or any large group.

Thirty respondents are not enough to give an accurate breakdown of the population at large, so you will have to fudge the figures some.

The survey should be made up of five questions asked two times: once in a bias-free way and once in a biased way. (See the student paper #1.) The first question in each pair should be biased. To hide the biasing as much as possible, the pairs of questions should not be asked together. You're to indicate the percentage of change you were able to effect in the respondents' answers from the biased questions to the bias-free ones. The math for this you will have to figure out. (Think how good this will be for you!) This percentage of change figure you are to use in paper number three.

Survey results are not always a reliable indication of how people feel about issues. How a survey is written can have a large impact on the responses. Statistics can be very deceiving, and it's tempting to have the opposition to what we believe presented as strong and dangerous, because it makes what we're doing that much more important.

An example of this can be found by looking at two surveys taken in 1992. A Roper Poll found that 22% of Americans—one in five—expressed doubts about the veracity of the Holocaust story. It made those groups who watch and\or refute the Holocaust revisionists that much more sensitive to how important their mission was becoming. But now the Gallup Organization, another polling company, is claiming that the number is 9% who doubt the truth of the Holocaust and only 4% say they were not sure.

One of the problems, according to Gallup, is one of language and meaning. Asking a question with a double negative can be confusing: "As you know, the term *Holocaust* usually refers to the killing of millions of Jews in Nazi death camps during World War II. Does it seem possible or does it seem impossible to you that the Nazi extermination of the Jews never happened?" A very poorly worded question indeed. Even the word *extermination* was a poor choice, for some people might think that could have meant total elimination, in which case the negative answer would have been appropriate. It might help you to understand this if you were to read the student paper #1 written for this exercise. Gallup asked 500 randomly selected people the Roper question and 500 randomly selected people their question worded this way: "Do you doubt that the Holocaust actually happened, or not?" This version produced very different results.

How a survey can be employed to benefit the people making it can be seen by a look at a few of the questions asked a few years ago of the residents of a county in Michigan before a vote was to be taken on a new contract for the college teachers. The teachers wanted more money, so the trustees sent a survey to the area residents. They then printed the results in the local newspaper, but they did not include the questions, which you will see were very biased. The biasing is so blatant that some of the respondents must have recognized it for what it was. Even the introduction gives the bias away. The excerpts here are reproduced exactly as they were sent to the taxpayers.

Notice the use of capital letters, references to the respondent being the owner of the school, references to the Board as the respondent's representative, the teachers as money-grubbers, the distortion of the figures about money, the position of virtue the Board takes, the placement and choice of options for the respondent, the appeal to a reasonable position (making the assumption that the respondent would agree) and the unfair choices the survey gives the respondent.

```
Dear Taxpayer:
```

> The junior college is **YOUR** college. As provided in the **Constitution and laws of Michigan,** we, the Board of Trustees, serve as **YOUR** elected representatives. . .operate and control the College for **YOU.** We want to know how you, the taxpayer, feel about key issues. . .

The words I have put in bold italics are the more obvious attempts by the Board to bias the respondent. The use of capital letters was by the school in the original survey.

1. The teachers union is *demanding* top salaries of over $19,000 per year for 36 weeks work. *Your Board* of Trustees believes this is *way too high.*
                    ( ) agree ( ) disagree

2. *Your Board* of Trustees believes the control of the College should *remain in the hands of the taxpayers* and that *YOUR Board of Trustees* should not negotiate *away control of the College.*
                    ( ) agree ( ) disagree

3. *Your Board* of Trustees believes *we* should keep expenditures within available income and should not agree to any settlement with the teachers union which would require *more taxes or deplete emergency* building repair funds.
                    ( ) agree ( ) disagree

33

5. *Your board* of Trustees believes a teacher should be hired or re-hired on merit only. We oppose any tenure clause in the contract which serves to **perpetuate incompetence.**

    ( ) agree ( ) disagree

6. Teachers at **your** junior college average $12,000 including fringe benefits for 38 weeks work. How many hours per week do you feel a teacher should spend in the classroom for this salary?:

    ( )less than 15( )15-20( )20-25( )25-30**( )more**

7. For 36 weeks work and 16 hours a week in the classroom, what do you feel a fair average salary should be?

    ( ) *Less than $5,000*   ( ) *$5,000 - $7,000*
    ( ) *$7,000 - $9,000*   ( ) *$9,000 - $12,000*
    ( ) *$12,000 - $15,000*   ( ) above $15,000

8. Will you support **your Board** of Trustees if we continue to **stand firm to protect your interests** regardless of the **pressures** the union leaders bring to bear?

    ( ) yes( ) no

Of course your questions will hide their bias much more carefully than these did. I have to laugh, even though it's years later, at how naive the administration of the college believed the residents of the county were. This is such a blatant attempt to influence the respondents to this survey, that I marvel at the line about perpetuating incompetence. But, you must understand that the job of the writer of a survey of this nature is to get the kind of responses that will support the writer's side of the controversy. Very few surveys are taken for the purpose of finding out what the respondents really think or feel. It's the results of the surveys that the writers want to use to support their positions. Below are some things you should keep in mind when you're ready to write your questions:

1. It's much easier to bias a response to an **opinion** question than it is to bias one asking for **factual information**. You should ask the respondents how they *feel* about the issues.

2. It's very hard to write bias-free questions. It will help you to write the five unbiased questions first, then to bias them.

3. Your bias-free questions will tend to be shorter than the biased ones—avoid this if you can, for it might tip off your reader.

4. Do not try to bias your questions enough to change every respondent's opinion, because the bias will then be obvious to many readers. If you change 15 to 20 percent of the responses, you will have done a good job.

5. Ways to bias questions:
   A. Imply one answer is better than another one—notice this technique in the first question in the example survey from the college.
   B. Suggest that it's in the interest of the respondent to answer a specific way. See question number nine in the example survey.
   C. Suggest the respondent, by a desired response, will be in agreement with the majority, the experts, the popular view or some patriotic group view. (See question two.)
   D. Introduce the question with information—notice this in question one and seven.

6. Your questions should ask for a *yes* or *no* answer.

7. If a respondent does not understand a question, the answer will not be valid—write the questions so the slowest thinker of the group will be able to understand them.

PAPER #2

The second paper is an argument paper designed to influence the reader to think in a specific way about a controversial issue. Ostensibly, the paper is to be an objective presentation of both sides of the question you've chosen to write about, but it is to use the following hidden biasing techniques to influence your readers.

1. Unequal number of arguments (one extra—hidden)
2. Use of words having known negative or positive connotations
3. Employment of knowledge of short term memory limitations
4. The use of sentence flow techniques. The arguments the writer wants the reader to accept should read easily, and the arguments on the other side should be written so as to be awkward and hard to read easily.
5. Placement of power technique. The last argument on the side the author favors should be much stronger than the last argument of the non-favored side.

INTRODUCTION:

The introduction should have a background that:
1. Gives a short history of the controversy: (see student paper, point #1)
2. Mentions the necessity of understanding the issues of the controversy: (see point #2)
3. Suggests that this will be an objective presentation of both sides of the question: (see point #3)
4. Breaks the controversy down into its issues. This is in the form of a process: (see point #4)

BODY

You have a choice of ways to set up the body:
1. You can present all of the arguments on one side of the question and then all of the

arguments on the other side: (see student paper #1)

2. You can present both sides of the question on each of the issues at the same time. Each of the issues is to be presented as a fully structured argument which will have four points: (See student paper #2, paragraph 5.)

1. A statement of the position
2. An explanation of the statement if needed
3. The supportive material
4. A conclusion

If the controversy has five issues, each one will be developed in this way. This is for both sides of the controversy.

CONCLUSION

The conclusion will:
1. Tie all of the issues together for both sides of the controversy
2. Mention the importance of the reader informing himself fully on the controversy
3. Ask the readers to decide for themselves how they feel about the controversy

PAPER #3

The third paper is to be an explanation of the process of biasing in writing and is to use your experiences in the first two papers as support for the statements you make about this subject. You're to use quotations taken from your first two papers as support for this paper: (see student paper #3)

BIASING NOTES

Exercise #2

The subject of the paper:

_____

The issues in the order of presentation:

1._____
2._____
3._____

4._____

5._____

6._____

The side of the question the reader should be influenced to agree with:

_____

The techniques used to bias the thinking of the reader:

1._____

2._____

3._____

4._____

5._____

PROPAGANDA

This exercise was created to help you to:

1. Recognize and understand the function of the eleven most common propaganda techniques used by writers
2. Write an effective piece of propaganda
3. Protect yourself against written propaganda by recognizing when it's being used to influence you

You will be writing a short piece of propaganda and an expository piece explaining how propaganda works.

As an example of the techniques used in propaganda, I have written a short satire of propaganda. You must understand that propaganda is not writers telling readers something they need to know or something which is true, or even partly true or is a fair way to give information. Propaganda is a well organized lie. Most organizations use propaganda to some extent. It's often seen by them as "putting the best forward." You will recognize this in action if you notice the information that the tobacco industry gives about the links between smoking and lung cancer. Once you recognize the techniques that propagandists use, you will be able to protect yourself against their words.

The following satire of propaganda makes the techniques very obvious. You will be able to pick them out. When I first used this example in my English class, some people got excited because they thought I was serious. They did not understand satire and they felt that I really thought Santa Claus was a bad person. Oh, well.

"The Devil's Advocate," a parody of propaganda, was written to demonstrate a number of techniques that are commonly found in the writings and speeches to which you're exposed. One or more of these may be found in most of the works of persuasive speakers/writers. "The Devil's Advocate" was written to make it easy for you to recognize what was being done to the reader. The examples found there of these techniques are exaggerations of them as they're used by serious propagandists. The techniques will be easy to find in "The Devil's Advocate" and some you will be able to find in "Let's Face the Truth—George" which appeared in our local paper.

Exercise #1

After studying the parody of propaganda use and the very funny satire of propaganda about George Washington, you're to write a piece of propaganda employing as many of the eleven techniques as you can. Choose your own subject. It can either be something in the news or an issue that you feel strongly about. You should not try to write satire or try to be funny. Do not worry about insulting anyone or appearing bigoted yourself—that is the nature of propaganda.

Exercise #2

You're to write an explanatory piece about the techniques used by propagandists. You're to use the information in this book and your own experiences writing propaganda to support the position you take in your paper.

PROPAGANDA TECHNIQUES

1. **Identify the Major Problem:**

   The writer often begins by identifying a problem and then talks of it as if there were no question about its importance to the reader.

2. **Give Evil Motives to Those Attacked:**

   The writers do not claim the act, person or group they attack is evil, but they imply as much. One way this is done is to label the possible evil motives of the person or group. Hitler did this when he wanted to propagandize against the Jews in the 1930's. He claimed all Jews were part of an international Jewish conspiracy, and he said further that they were members of an inferior race. He claimed they were motivated by greed for power and money.

   Senator McCarthy did the same thing in the 1950's when he attacked the State Department for harboring communists. He claimed many members of the State Department were motivated by a desire to overthrow the government of the United States.

   There are religious leaders in the world who claim that people who do not think as they do are motivated by the Devil. Some of the religious leaders in the Mid-East feel that Christians are unclean and motivated by Evil. Large businesses claim unions are motivated by a desire to take power away from corporations, destroy initiative, and subvert capitalism. Communists claim capitalists want to dominate the world and destroy the opportunity for workers to have good lives. A close examination of the writers' motives often shows them to be exactly those which they attribute to their targets.

3. **Suggest Guilt by Inference and Negative Assumption:**

The writer implies the attacked person or group is guilty of (whatever) by claiming an association or relationship between the person or group attacked and some mutually agreed upon evil. "If Bill is in favor of not banning books, he must be in favor of pornography." "If Betty is in favor of woman's liberation, she must be in some doubt about her own sexuality." "If John doesn't stand up for the 'Pledge of Allegiance,' he must be a communist."

Propagandists suggest that the issues are so clear that the choices must be either all for or all against. Things are either black or white. There's no room for any other conclusion than the ones they have come to. They deny all evidence and experience which might lead to conclusions other than their own, such as John's desire not to stand being motivated by his religious beliefs.

4. **"Recognized Good" as Motives for Attack:**

Writers claim to be motivated by values they know are popular with their readers, thereby impugning the motives of the attacked person or group. "Because I am one-hundred percent American and I attack him, he must be less than one-hundred percent American and motivated by some anti-American value." They set up their own criteria as a standard of what is right and wrong. "I love children and want to protect them from harm, so if he doesn't agree with everything I say about burning books, he must not love children."

5. **Substitute Questions for Evidence:**

If writers cannot prove the attacked persons or groups guilty of something, they ask questions in such a way that they imply the answers would prove the guilt. "The man is forty-three years old, and he has never married. Let me ask you: Why? He doesn't belong to any club, he doesn't have any friends we know about, he is never seen with anyone, but he spends lots of time watching the schoolboys practice football. Why is this? Does this man sound like the kind of man we want to have for a scout leader?" By employing this technique, even the most innocent act can be made to seem suspect.

6. **Claim Guilt by Symbolic Association:**

There have been and are powerful symbols in our culture which have been seen as both positive and negative, depending on who observed them. There was a time, not too long ago, when women schoolteachers couldn't wear red dresses, men who wore beards were seen as evil and young men who wore long hair were thought of as troublemakers.

Propagandists link the attacked person or group with objects they know their readers see as negative symbols. Religious leaders in Iran link women in slacks and short dresses with

Western Infidels. Woman's liberationists have been linked to tennis shoes, African-Americans with watermelon and ghetto blasters, capitalists with cigars, revolutionists with beards and combat clothes, small town Chambers of Commerce members with green leisure suits and\or white shoes and belts. "I wouldn't say she hates men, but she always wears slacks, sensible shoes, never puts her hair up, wears no makeup, and she carries a book around with her all the time. Now that by itself don't mean a whole lot, but there has to be something wrong with a girl who don't like a slightly off-color joke now and then." This kind of stereotyping makes it easy for the propagandists to lump into a large negatively identified group, diverse peoples and behaviors and make them seem to have a common, threatening aspect.

7. Imply Co-Interest:

Writers who successfully propagandize, suggest their readers and they have the same values, goals and desires. Hitler appealed to the pride the German people had in Germany and told them he felt the same pride. The people who would ban books in a library talk of their love of kids. The political leaders of all countries who want to go to war appeal to the patriotic feelings of their people: "A war to make the world safe for democracy," "A popular struggle for the freedom loving peoples of North Vietnam," "Since we all love peace, this will be a war to end all wars." Listen to the bigot here: "We both want the same thing, we want our women safe to walk on the street without being spoke to by one of them. We got this meeting tonight. You think just like we do and we need a man like you to help us. You can even use my sheet." The implication is, of course, the reader feels the same way the writer does—any right thinking person has to have the same interests "we" do.

8. Identify Threats From Without:

Writers suggest that the danger has been imported. They're appealing to tribal instinct. During the voter registration drives in the south in the 60's many of the police and politicians blamed the troubles on "outside agitators." The idea is to suggest that "We" don't have a problem, "They" have the problem and have brought it to us. "Sure we have drugs in the school, but they're brought here by the dropouts and older kids." Or, "Our union members were happy till those outside agitators came here."

Just before he invaded Poland, Hitler told the German people that the Poland was going to attack. In our recent past there were military and political leaders who advocated dropping the atom bomb on China so the Chinese wouldn't get strong enough to destroy America.

Does this sound familiar? "We have to support a South American dictatorship because, if we don't the Russians will take over." We would rather have a home-grown dictator run a repressive government than have our neighbors influenced by outsiders. In a satiric fictional study, *The Iron Mountain Report*, published in the late 60's, the point was made that if our leaders didn't have the Russians to use as a threat to maintain a unified American consciousness, it would be necessary to invent a threat from outer space in order to keep the people of this country working together. The thrust of this report was that people are easier to control if they're asked to unify against a potential foreign threat than if they're asked to work for a common good.

9. **Demand Pre-Conclusion Agreement:**

Writers want a positive response from their readers\listeners before they ask them to agree with their main points. Remember The Music Man in the play by the same name ends his song with "We have trouble right here in River City." He starts with questions, each of which can be answered with a "Yes" response. "Does your son roll his knickers above the knee? does he say, `So's your old man?'" the writers want their readers used to answering in the affirmative before they propose their big questions.

10. **Use of Urgent Tone:**

Writers speak as if the problems must be solved now. If the decision to agree with them and act as they direct is not made now, there will be dire consequences. There must be a pressing need to act, and this has to be communicated to the readers. "If we don't act now before it's too late. . ." "Now is the time for all men to stand up and be counted . . ." "Unless we all agree and work together to solve this problem now. . ."

Propagandists want their readers to act before they have time to think out the positions the writers have given them. "Write your congressman now." "Can we afford another generation of illiterate children?" "It's not too late to stop the effects of pollution, but we must act now." "If one country in Southeast Asia falls, the rest will fall. We must stop this spread now."

11. **Concluding With An Assumption of Conviction:**

Writers end their propaganda with the attitude that they have convinced their readers of their positions. There can be no thought that the positions are weak or that a thinking person, once presented with the facts, might disagree with them.

In the following satire of propaganda techniques, the techniques are labeled T (#) to correspond to the above listing.

The Devil's Advocate

T (1) I put it to you that there are some suspect aspects to Santa Claus. There are some things that aren't right. *T (2)* Here we have an elderly man who is inordinately fond of children, young children. *T (3)* He lives with a woman called Mrs. Claus. Nowhere in the literature is there a record of their marriage or where she comes from. There are no children. *T (5)* Could she be his sister? Or, instead of incestuous relationships, do we have to look for Oedipal possibilities? *T (2 & 3)* If this bearded man is still living with his mother and likes small boys and girls, does this not fit a familiar pattern? *T (3)* If these two are not married, what sort of role models are they?

T (6) The color red long has had a vile connotation for most of us. Yet, this man flaunts red colors in his clothing. *T (2)* Even his surrogates are found wearing red in malls and department stores, holding onto and whispering to other people's little children. And giving them candy! And promising them gifts!

T (3 & 4) In many of our churches we are warned against consorting with the Devil. *T (6)* The Devil wears red. The devil has pointed ears. Have you seen the pictures of Santa's helpers? Have you noticed their ears? Pointed! We are told the Devil has familiars who have strange and supernatural powers. What of Rudolph? *T (6)* His red nose! He flies! He sings songs in English yet! If this isn't supernatural and suspect, I don't know what is.

T (7) We have been warned about the International Communist Conspiracy corrupting our children.

T (3) We have known for a long time that sugar—like that found in candy canes—can change the behavior of children. This is the manipulation of children's minds through behavioral conditioning. Is this American? That doesn't even sound nice. What color do we associate with the communists? Right, red! Doesn't look so good now, does it?

T (7 & 8) And what about the American capitalist way of life? Where do all his toys come from? Not Sears. Not Penny's. Some workshop at the North Pole. Foreign imports! What does this do to the balance of payments? *T (7 & 8)* What about American jobs? We have unemployment in this great country of ours, and he uses slave labor and exports his goods in the dead of night. *T (5)* In secret! What about flying right over customs officers at the border crossings? Does he cheat on his import duties? *T (7)* You know he does! I know he does. Who complains? Nobody.

We have to ask ourselves some questions. *T (5 & 9)* Is there a conspiracy of silence at this time of year? Have you seen adults whispering more lately? Have you heard of secret, hidden lists. Are children denied knowledge about their own futures? Are threats of reprisal more common lately? Are things as good now as they were four months ago? Do we have a problem?

T (10) You bet we do, and it's serious.

I gave this satire to some students one year near Christmas vacation and, it may be hard for you to believe, but I had some parents get upset when they read this parody of propaganda. Many people are very unsophisticated in their reading and are quite easy to manipulate. You, after having read through the listing of techniques, recognize what this piece is, but, even as outrageous as it is, some people are still affected by it.

Here is another fun piece of propaganda. This is also a satire on the techniques. This one appeared about February 14th in a small town paper.

Let's Face The Truth—George Washington Was A Vandal

With George Washington's birthday at hand, it's time to re-examine the matter of the cherry tree.

Over the years, the first president of the United States has received much acclaim for telling the truth and admitting that he chopped down the cherry tree.

"Father, I cannot tell a lie"—Washington's quaint response to his father's cross-examination—has become engraved on the collective American consciousness as a glorious example of incorruptible integrity.

But the fact that he did in fact chop down said tree—a brutish act of mindless vandalism—is blithely swept under the rug.

It takes a long time to grow a cherry tree. The cherry tree belonged not to Washington but to Washington's dad. It was a cheap, gutless trick to chop it down.

If George Washington had lived in a society that wasn't so soft on crime, the story would be retold today as the occasion when the right hand of the future president of the United States of America was justly severed in retribution for his heinous crime.

In my opinion, this disgusting episode should be stricken from the record of American folklore. It sets a terrible precedent for the youth of this great nation, goading them to wantonly destroy property, encouraging them in the belief that they can get by with it simply by repeating the wretched formula, "Father, I cannot tell a lie."

But the truly appalling feature of this sordid tale is the threat it poses for our national security by exalting the poisonous idea that it's good to tell the truth.

Honesty may be admirable in common folk, but in politicians it's a flaw that raises questions about fitness for office. Where would our government's capabilities to deceive, confuse, baffle and distort be if our politicians were incompetent liars? How could we sow disinformation and keep our enemies guessing if we had a chief executive who was forever babbling, "I cannot tell a lie"?

Unless our government can freely deny that it's doing what it's doing and promise to do what it has no intention of doing, its hands are tied. How can we hope to compete with the Russians if our country is run by a bunch of Boy Scouts enslaved to truth? Candidates for office should be required to take a lie detector test to prove their aptitude for lying.

Now is the time for soul-searching. We need to ask ourselves some serious questions. What kind of parents were the Washingtons to let their child play with axes? What kind of nation elects a vandal to its highest office?

Can we afford to continue venerating Washington's heinous crime? Isn't it just a matter of time before aspiring politicians run amok with axes chopping down cherry trees just to provide them with a media event for confessing the truth?

It doesn't require much imagination to see the direction this country is headed: deforestation, a fatal decline in oxygen levels, not to speak of the extinction of the cherry crop and the tragic demise of the banana split as we know it today.

Before it's too late, I humbly propose that the evidence of Washington's honesty be suppressed. Let us rehabilitate the myth of our first president, depicting him as a facile liar, a Machiavellian serpent who shrewdly deceived his dad like any healthy American kid would do. Let's rewrite the story of the cherry tree.

"I cannot tell a lie, Pops. Benjamin Franklin chopped down your cherry tree. I tried to stop him, but he wouldn't listen to me. I hope you'll teach him a lesson he'll never forget."

You should be able to pick out many of the listed techniques from this piece also.

In your explanatory paper you will have to decide the point you want to make. You can decide that the techniques are not effective or that they are a powerful tool. The process can either be developed from the list of techniques propagandists use supported by examples, or you can use the two propaganda pieces supported by the techniques. You might want to find your own propaganda piece to use with the one you write to support your expository paper.

PROPAGANDA NOTES

1. The subject of the propaganda piece:

_____

_____

_____

2. How the reader should feel about the subject after reading the propaganda:

_____

3. The intended audience: Age:_____ Education: _____

   Socio-economic position: _____
4. About this subject, the majority of people in this group feel that:

   _____

5. The major fears or anxieties connected with this topic that this group has:

   1._____
   2._____
   3._____
   4._____
   5._____
   6._____

   The techniques planned for use in this piece:

   1._____
   2._____
   3._____
   4._____
   5._____
   6._____

TERM PAPER

This exercise was designed to help you learn to:
1. Structure a term paper
2. Follow a style sheet
3. Use primary research
4. Appreciate that a term paper is much more than just copying material from books and magazines
5. Understand that research can be interesting

In the past you may have done what I and most of the adults you know have done when we were told that we had to write a term paper. We collected a pile of books and copied sections that related to our topic. We then strung the copied-out parts together with some sort of continuity and turned the whole mess in, hoping that our teachers would not have time enough to check to see if maybe we had just changed some of the paragraphs and sentences around and omitted putting in the quotation marks.

This may have taught us something about putting a term paper together but not much about writing or about the subject.

In this exercise you will be restricted to primary research, which means that you will be able to include something in your paper only if you researched it yourself.

Since your paper will have to deal with some aspects of your town, you will be restricted to local resources—those you can find that deal with your community.

Primary research may include looking at original documents, but may not include what others have said about them. You can use old yearbooks from your town's schools, your village or town charter, local ordinances or laws, locally written histories of your town or the people in it, newspaper accounts of local events, court house records of land ownership and deed transfers, photographs you take, old photographs of your town not in books about your town, surveys, conversations you've had with local people like the librarian, mayor, police chief, business manager, zoning board president, or elderly citizens who might be able to tell you some of the history of your town. What you can't use is something that someone else has written on your subject.

There is no one way to write a term paper. When you get to college, you will be given style sheets to use by the departments if they require you to write such papers. If this is not the case, you should ask any instructor who assigns a term paper, which style sheet you should use, and you should follow it exactly. For this exercise, there should be a number of books about writing term papers and style sheets in the public library that you will be able to follow.

To get a subject for this paper you may have to interview a number of people. You might think about subjects like: your town passing a millage vote for a new school, re-paving the streets, a group of local businessmen organizing to fight the building of a mall just outside of town, the financing or building of a city park or efforts to re-zone areas for an industrial park.

MAGAZINE EVALUATION

This exercise has been designed to help you learn:
1. Ways to judge the readership level of any magazine
2. Relationships between sections of the reading public and the magazines they read
3. Methods of incorporating classifications you make of groups of objects and/or people into supportive material for your writing of explanatory expositions

There's a tremendous diversity of interests in this country catered to by the publishers of magazines. There are at least five thousand periodicals published monthly, though only a few of these have a wide enough readership to justify their being on the racks in bookstores. A bookstore might display sixty to one hundred titles, which still gives the average reader a large selection.

This exercise will give you an opportunity to present, in an explanatory paper, a process by which a potential purchaser might select a magazine which would be satisfying and consistent with his or her reading level and interest.

For the purposes of this paper, the magazine-reading public and the magazines available to them will have to be roughly grouped into categories of high, middle and low. Of course, this rough grouping is not accurate, but to be much more exact would make the writing of this paper impossibly complicated. These arbitrary groupings will not indicate value judgments on your part, nor should they be seen by your reader as such. The magazines in the low category are as good for the purposes for which they're intended as are those in the high category. So, try to avoid saying that any one magazine is best, or that one level is better than any other one.

This examination will not include the categorizing of individuals of the magazine-reading public, but will restrict itself to the examination of magazines and the placing of them into groups which are appropriate for different groups of readers. To do this, of course, magazine readers also will have to be grouped, and these groups will be determined by the group's socio-economic and educational/intellectual levels. Once you've set up these three categories of readership, high, middle and low, it then remains only to place the magazines available to them into high, middle and low groups in order to demonstrate to the reader of your paper that there's a usable relationship between the readers of magazines and the magazines they buy. This paper will establish that relationship by giving your reader the means to quickly determine the level of any magazine.

Most libraries do not carry those magazines which would fall into the low level, so you might have to find old copies in the beauty parlor or a neighbor's home. There are a number of magazines, which in this paper will be classified as low, which are not considered pornographic by some people, but, it might be wise to stay away from the *Playboy* and *Penthouse* types. In fact you might find offensive many of the covers on low level magazines such as the detective and crime magazines. If this is the case, then don't use them and pick, using your new understanding of how to judge, some low level magazines which do not offend you or will not offend your parents.

The one-subject magazines like *Road and Track, Skiing* and *Flying* will not work too well for this paper because they appeal to all levels of readers. For the same reason, you should also avoid teenage and ethnic magazines.

There's a very small group of high and low level magazines and a great number of middle level ones. There's really more diversity in the large middle group than there is between the middle and either end. These problems will have to be ignored.

The placing of magazine readers into levels is accomplished by dividing the readers on the basis of their:
1. Social standings
2. Economic positions
3. Educational levels
4. Intellectual abilities

The criteria by which magazines are placed into high, middle and low groups are:
1. The qualities and types of art on the covers
2. Advertisements
3. Letters to the editors
4. Tables of content
5. Paper qualities

A magazine may be placed in its level by its cover art. Notice:

1. High level covers of *Smithsonian, Architectural Digest* and *The New Yorker* have excellent photography, nicely balanced colors and figures, non-intrusive lettering and tasteful subject matter dealing with art, design, literature and travel.

2. Middle level covers deal with politics, home decorating, family life and news. The photography is still of high quality, but the subject matter is aimed more at the average householder. The colors are brighter, and on most middle level magazines there are blurbs on the covers advertising the contents. The art work is not as finely balanced and there's more use of human models.

50

3. Low level magazines are sold like soap is sold, by having bright colors on the covers—notice how the attractive yellows, reds and blues used on low level covers are the same shades as are used on Tide, Cheer and Borax. The subjects deal almost exclusively with sex and\or violence. The photography and printing are generally of poor quality—fuzzy and out of balance. The models look well used and are usually in provocative poses. On the covers which depict violence, the guns and knives are always placed so as to be easily seen. The art work is covered with content blurbs which relate poorly with the magazines' contents.

The readers of high level magazines choose the ones they do because they're familiar with their contents. This is somewhat true of the readers of middle level magazines, but the readers of low level magazines choose the ones they do because of the pictures on the covers or the blurbs which catch their interest.

Advertisements are another quick way to determine intended readership. Notice:

1. High level magazines sell expensive items—Steuben ashtrays at $1,500 or men's watches at $37,000. The ads are often full page and in color. There are few words—many times they have only the retail outlets' names or the designers' names. It's obvious that these items are advertised in magazines intended for people who have money.

    It's not always true, but generally in America, money, intelligence, education and social position are related, and we would expect to find this relatedness in magazines also.

2. Middle level magazines advertise items of interest to the great majority of Americans—washing machines, beer, cigarettes, clothes, cleaning agents, cars and insurance. Often there are full page ads, but the art work is not nearly as fine, there's much more advertising copy (words) and more monochrome or non-color ads. The cost of the merchandise is affordable for people making forty to eighty thousand dollars a year.

3. Advertisements in low level magazines are never in color, are usually small, are for low cost goods, and are designed to appeal to people with low income and little education. The people who are attracted to low level magazines believe in the printed word and are impressed by it, so, many of the ads have lots of copy. Certainly, any man who has an education, social position and a good job will not be attracted by an advertisement for a free shoe sales kit or a course in how to be a private detective.

The letters to the editors in all magazines deal with the articles in previous issues, but there is a great difference in the letters. Notice:

1. High level magazines have letters to the editors, which, in a fairly objective way, present the writers' views. The sentence structuring, length, diction and attitude indicate the writers' intelligence and education. Seldom do the writers begin with, "I enjoy your

51

magazine, but. . . ." The writers' names are included with the letters, and many are recognizable as belonging to prominent people. They're often from teachers in universities, leaders in industry or people who serve in governmental positions.

2. Letters to the editors in middle level magazines are harder to categorize because of the wide range of interests and abilities of the middle group. The people in the high end of the middle group write much like the people do in the upper group, and the people in the low end of the middle group write much like the people do in the low group of readers. Generally, the medium level letter writers write in a more personal way than do the people in the high group. The letters tend to be shorter and the vocabulary level is close to that which is found in *Reader's Digest*.

3. Low level magazine letters to the editors are quite short, very subjective and have a petulant or "Wow, you saved my life," attitude. They read like they might have been written with crayon on the backs of envelopes or grocery bags. They're often signed with just initials and a city—"E.F. Detroit." They're not ungrammatical, so they have been either heavily edited or were written by staffers at the magazines. They almost always contain high praise for the magazines and often thank the publishers for the fine job they do.

The tables of content in magazines are a good indication of the interests of their readers. Notice:
1. High level magazines' tables of content deal with art, literature, finance, travel, theater, music and dance.

2. Middle level magazines' tables of content deal with things of interest to that large group of middle level people: international affairs, politics, schools, taxes, instructions in how to do or make things, clothing, children, food and decorating.

3. Low level magazines' tables of content deal with sex and violence. The low level magazines are much more moral in tone than are the higher levels, but this would be hard to tell by the titles of the articles.

As a general rule, better quality magazines are printed on high quality paper. There are, of course, exceptions to this. There are some highly intellectual magazines printed on pulp paper, and some very low level magazines printed on slick paper, but for the purposes of your examination, the rule is valid if you mention that there are exceptions.

The points made in your paper should be accompanied by examples cut from magazines. Because most magazine covers and full page ads are larger than theme paper, it will be necessary to crop or fold in some cases to avoid having mouse sandwiches—tails and ends sticking out. All of the examples should not be together at the end of the paper but should accompany the texts they illustrate.

Remember, this paper should not make value judgements about either the buyers or the magazines. The placement of either in the high or low category is only a labeling convenience and does not indicate worth or value.

As you select your magazines to use as examples, you should realize that you can use just one magazine for the example in each level. If this is the case, you should find one that is characteristic of that level and you should tell your reader that there are a number of magazines in that level but that the one you're using as an example is characteristic of that group.

You might want to use a number of magazines for each level and pick out representative samples for the points you're making about the levels of the magazines. All high level magazines don't have letters to the editors, and you might have to find examples in another high level magazine. If this is the case, your reader should be told this.

Be careful when you select the low level magazine. The intent in this paper is not to have you experience reading matter which is not suitable for you, but to give you two things: 1) a way to judge reading matter suitable for you, and 2) give you material for the writing of an explanatory exposition. You can accomplish both of these goals without reading material that you or your parents might find offensive.

CONTENTION:

The contention for an explanatory exposition must come from a conclusion you've come to from your examination of the material you're going to explain. In this case you've examined a number of magazines and have come to the conclusion that there is a relationship between the levels of sophistication of the magazines and the levels of their intended readership.

The contention for this paper then might read: ***It is possible by quickly looking through a magazine to tell for whom it was written.***

PROCESS:

The process for any explanatory exposition is derived from a decision made about the order of the supportive material used. The key words in your process sentence will present you with a way to key your reader into that order. All you need in any process statement is a sentence with a listing of the key words in the same order you plan on using to present the material. The process sentence for this paper is fairly complicated because you have two things you have to organize—the readership of magazines and the magazines that readership might choose. There are two good ways to structure this process:

1. Divide the body into three parts: high, middle and low, and have each of these parts supported by aspects of the magazines' cover art, advertisements etc.

53

2. Divide the body into five parts: cover art, advertisements, letters to the editors, tables of content and paper qualities, and for each of these divisions, present examples of high, middle and low level magazines.

With either choice of structuring the body, the criteria by which the magazine reading public is divided into the three groups: high, middle and low, needs to be explained to the reader. The list of four deciding conditions will not be part of the process because it will not be part of the supportive material in the body, so it should be placed before the contention or between the contention and the process. If these criteria were to be placed between the contention and the process, this part of the introduction might read like this: (**contention**) *It is possible, by quickly glancing through a magazine, to tell for whom it was written.* (**the method of dividing the magazine reading public**) *The magazine reading public, divided into three groups, high, middle and low, based on their socio-economic positions and their intellectual/educational levels,* (**process statement**) *has magazines available to it which can be similarly divided, based on the art on the covers, advertisements, letters to the editors, tables of content and paper qualities.*

BODY

If the body of your paper is to be split into three sections: high, middle and low, for the levels of magazines, each of the sections should begin with an introduction to that level of magazine and some general statement about what the reader could expect to find there.

If you plan to use one or two magazines to demonstrate the characteristics of each level, the magazines should be presented to your reader as representative examples of their level. This part of the body might read: *High level magazines are generally published for intelligent people who have good educations and good incomes. A typical high level publication,* Smithsonian, *has been used to illustrate the characteristics of this group of sophisticated and slick magazines.*

1. The magazines to be used in the paper:

High: _____ _____

Med: _____ _____

Low: _____ _____

2. The conclusion you've come to about classifying magazines:

_____

_____

_____

_____

3. Your contention based on this conclusion:

_____

_____

_____

_____

4. There will be at least two parts to the process—the three levels of magazines and those parts of the magazines that can be used to put them in one of the levels.

The key words to be used in the process:

1. _____ 2. _____

3. _____ 4. _____

5. _____ 6. _____

APPENDIX

The following papers were written by high school students whom I had the pleasure of working with for four years in an experimental program at a college preparatory level. They were given the choice to take part in the experiment and were given that same choice each year. Those who elected to stay in my English level for the four years turned out to be exceptional writers. As you can tell by these papers, I have a right to be proud of them. These papers have not been edited to be placed here. They're reproduced just as they were turned in to me in the classroom.

Niles High School
Library Manual

by

Xxx Xxxxx

Table of Contents

page 1

Rules of the Niles High School Library

1. Do not disturb other people—be quiet.
2. Library materials should be kept neat and clean.
3. Return all materials to proper places.
4. Check out materials in your own name.
5. Return books on date due.

Hours

7:15 AM to 3:45 PM Monday through Friday

page 2

Floor Plan of Library

Here was drawn a floor plan of the library

Dewey Decimal System

Explanation

1) Books on same subject have the same level numbers.
2) Ten main groups of subjects. Divided into ten subgroups, etc.

Ten Main Groups

000 General Works - books on library work, encyclopedias and journalism
100 Philosophy - psychology, occult, ethics
200 Religion - Bible, books about the Bible, mythology, Christianity, world religions
300 Social Sciences - government, politics, education, commerce, stamp collecting, manners and customs, family etiquette
400 Language - grammar, style, foreign languages, Ex. Spanish, Latin, French
500 Science - general science, ex. math, chemistry, physics, astronomy, also insects, reptiles and birds
600 Technology - medicine, drugs, electronics, engineering, radio and television, aviation, agriculture, home economics, business, manufacturers, manual training.
700 Arts - sculpture, painting, photography, music, sports, hobbies, games.
800 Literature - American, English, poetry, plays.
900 History - geography and travel, biography, histories of countries.

Ex. of subdivision numbering

400 - Language - Spanish 460, English 420, German 430, French 440.

CARD CATALOG (explanation)

Card Catalog - Used to find books by alphabetical order

CARD CATALOG

Location - Refer to floor map page 2.

Ex. of cards in card catalog (non-fiction)

Example of non-fiction card

Fiction Books

Location - Refer to floor map, p. 2

How to find:
1. Look in card catalog under title, subject or author of book. (See card catalog p. 5)
2. Find section of books in library where that book would be found.
Return - Refer to p. 15 under Fiction books
How to check out:
1. Sign name on card in book
2. Librarian will stamp book and card
3. Librarian keeps card
Fines - refer to p. 14 under Fiction Books

Filmstrips

Location - refer to floor map, p. 2

How to find:
1. Look in card catalog under title, subject, or author of filmstrip. (Refer to card catalog p ?????)
2. Look in gray cabinets in audio room (refer to floor map.)

Check out: Refer to p. 7 under Filmstrips.

How to check out:
1. Sign name on white magazine slip at front desk.

Magazine _____

Date of Magazine _____

Your Name _____

Today's Date _____ Date Due _____

1st Hour Teacher _____

Return - Refer to p. 15 under Filmstrips.
fines - Refer to p. 14 under Filmstrips.

GENERAL REFERENCE

Location - Refer to floor map p. 2
How to find - Look in card catalog under type of reference.
Check out - Refer to p. 6 under General Reference.
How to check out - Same as for fiction Books p. 6
Return - Refer to p. 15 under General Reference.

LIST OF GENERAL REFERENCES

Encyclopedia
Dictionary
Almanac
Who's Who
General Science
Facts

INFORMATION FILE

Location - Refer to floor map p. 2

List of Materials in Information File
Non-inventoried material
Current events - paper clippings
Magazine articles (current)
Pamphlets

Check out - Use magazine slip.

Magazine _____

Date of Magazine _____

Your Name _____

Today's Date _____ Date Due _____

1st Hour Teacher _____

Return - refer to p. 15

Fines - Refer to p. 14 under Information File.

MAGAZINES

Location - Refer to p. 2 - floor map

Check out - Refer to p. 15 under Magazines

How to check out - Use Magazine slip.

Magazine _____

Date of Magazine _____

Your Name _____

Today's Date _____ Date Due _____

1st Hour Teacher _____

Return - Refer to p. 15
Fines - Refer to p. 14 under Magazines

HOW TO FIND AN ARTICLE

Refer to *Reader's Guide to Periodical Literature*

Look up by subject:

An example of a subject listing

(example)

Or, look up by author:

An example of an author listing

(example)

Note: Guide to abbreviations are found in front of *Reader's Guide to Periodical Literature*

Non-Fiction Books

Location:
    Refer to floor map - pg 2

How to find:
    Use card catalog to find.
    Look under subject, title, or author.

Checkout:
    Refer to pg. 12 under Non-Fiction Books.

How to check out:
    1) Sign name on card in book.
    2) Librarian or aid will stamp it.
    3) Librarian or aid keeps card.

Return:
    Refer to pg. 15

Fines:
    Refer to pg. 14 under Non-Fiction Books.

Visual Aids

Location:
    Refer to Librarian.

List of Visual Aids:
1) record players	4) screens
2) projectors	5) tapes
3) overheads	6) tape recorders

Check out:
    Refer to pg. 12 under Visual Aids.

How to check out:
    1) Sign name on sheet at librarian's desk.
    2) Tell how long you will have Visual Aid.

Return:
    Refer to pg. 15

Fines:
    Refer to pg. 14 under Visual Aids.

Fines for Library Materials

Fiction Books:

1st week overdue - notice
2nd week overdue - 5 cents a day
3rd week overdue - 10 cents a day
4th week overdue - referral

Non-Fiction Books:

1st week overdue - notice
2nd week overdue - 5 cents a day
3rd week overdue - 10 cents a day
4th week overdue - referral
Five cents per day overdue for:
Filmstrips
General Reference
Information File Material
Magazines
Maps
Newspapers
Visual Aid Materials
No fine - librarian will come to look for you.

Checkout times for Materials

Fiction and Non-Fiction Books - 2 weeks
Filmstrips - overnight
General Reference - overnight
Information File Materials - overnight
Magazines - overnight
Maps - overnight
Newspapers - None
Visual Aid Material - duration of sign out

Return of Library Materials

Return to front desk.

Maps

Location - In map file - Refer to floor plan pg. 2
How to find a map - rummage through them. Not listed in card catalog.
Check out - refer to pg. 16 under Maps.
How to check out - Use magazine slip:

Magazine _____

Date of Magazine _____

Your Name _____

Today's Date _____ Date Due _____

1st Hour Teacher _____

Return - Refer to pg. 15
Fines - Refer to pg. 14 under Maps.

EXERCISE 3

What is Fair?

Americans' concepts of fairness have been formed over many years of history. These concepts have been changed and modified to suit the current society and lifestyle. The idea of fairness has evolved through the years with the influence of Hammurabi's Code, which served as the first set of written laws, the chivalric codes of the middle ages, and even the organized competitive sports of today. Although *fairness* can be defined, the definition may be different among different people. One definition is: An impartial, unprejudiced, way of judgement or distribution. If it were possible to impose this concept of fairness on the entire world, my life would be very difficult and would be very changed. My life would be changed in about every aspect of it because everyone in the world would have same amount of everything.

It would be hard to get used to my new way of life because, for one thing, I wouldn't have many of the things I take for granted right now. The biggest change, or at least most noticeable would be food intake. If I were to list the foods I normally eat in an average day, I would find the list would have to be cut in half to be fair. There would be no junk food such as candy bars, cakes, desserts, and other sweets at all. I would only be eating enough to keep me alive and that would be it. An example of a day before and after the making of everything fair would look like this.

Before Imposed Concept	After Imposed Concept
Breakfast: 2 slices of toast, butter, hot cereal, milk, orange juice, eggs, sausage	Breakfast: Some kind of of cereal, grain (oatmeal) some drink (water)
Lunch: sandwich, meat, milk, salad, dessert	Lunch: bread (maybe) salad, some drink (water)
Dinner: meat dish, mashed potatoes vegetable, bread, milk, butter, vegetable	Dinner: bread, some drink, grain substitute, water

Comparing the two charts, a very noticeable difference is in meat. There wouldn't be much meat and therefore, people would eat mainly vegetables or grain. There wouldn't be any milk because people would be eating grain and there would be nothing for the cows to eat. There would be a lot of malnutrition in the world and people's bones and teeth would be affected by the absence of calcium.

I would also lose many of my clothes, although I don't think I would be hurt that much if I were to only have two pairs of pants and three shirts. I would have a jacket and a pair of shoes also.

In the way of shelter, every house would have only two rooms. A family of four would live in with their average number of pets. That number is one dog, cat, or goldfish. The house would be furnished with three pieces of furniture, a couch, chair, table and bed. All four family members would sleep in the same bed because there would be only one house per family.

As for luxury items and appliances, they would be very few in number. There would be one telephone for each city block, and only one television for each 200 people. Every other family would have a radio, and each city would have one car for people to use. Every house would be located on a plot of land measuring .045 square miles.

Education would really hurt me since the average educational level for the world is about third grade. The highest academic level that people could reach would be third grade. Therefore, there would be no colleges or even high schools. Everyone would do the jobs they would be capable of doing. There would be no doctors, lawyers, or any other professional people.

If I were to live to the average age, I would die at the age of 54.

If there were a way to make the world fair, nothing would be the same, in my life or anyone's. For me it would be a change for the worse, but the less fortunate would end up better off. Food, shelter, and education would be the most obvious changes but the list of differences could go on and on forever. One, thing is for sure. The next time I say something isn't fair, I'll think about it and ask myself, "Do I want things to be fair?"

EXERCISE #4

Book Covers

Being an author, I have often wondered if there is a secret to selling books. Obviously, the story line, characters, style, and writer's skill are all important factors, but is there some sure-fire method of selling a book quickly and conveniently to the consumer? After all, most people, when buying a book, don't read two or three chapters to determine whether the story is of interest to them. Instead, they usually skim the front and back covers and base their decisions on what they see there. So, it would seem reasonable that you can tell a book by its cover material. To demonstrate the validity of this idea, various parts of the cover material of paperback books such as cover art, teasers, book reviews, publishers and number of re-printings have been examined.

Because there are so many different types of books that a person can read, it is almost impossible to talk about every kind of cover material and all of the characteristics that are specific to each. However, certain patterns can be observed and used as indicators when searching for a book. Romance, science fiction, adventure, sports, western, and fantasy are examples of different varieties of writing, all of which can be further divided into smaller groups that vary in sophistication. For example, the cover art found on an unsophisticated sports story such as *Relief Pitcher* written for a fifth grade reader is very similar to the cover art of a typical romance novel such as *Midnight Passion*. Therefore, you could conclude that typical romance novels are written for unsophisticated readers at about the fifth grade reading level. Most cover art of romance, adventure, and sports stories that are written on a low level have pictures of a man or woman or both engaged in whatever activity the book is about. For instance, romance books almost always have a good looking man and a beautiful woman embracing or kissing each other. A mystery romance would have the same theme, except usually there is no man, only a woman running from a castle or an evil looking house in the background. The typical romance books such as those published by Harlequin are brightly colored in pastels and the people's features resemble those of a Barbie doll's. The balance of art is most often very poor and sometimes there are images of different objects such as beautiful houses, sports cars, or handsome men all thrown together in fuzzy collages.

Another type of art you can identify quite easily by a quick glance is on science fiction novels and short stories, which are very popular today. Generally, the art deals with a futuristic theme. There may be a picture of unusual spacecraft, aliens, or any other subject dealing with space travel and technical advances that are as of now, not invented or discovered. The coloring of this art ranges from the very subtle shades of sophisticated science fiction to brilliant tones and colors found on the less sophisticated covers. Also, the art is often concerned with machinery and technical equipment rather than people. Sometimes the art is of an abstract nature made up of intricate patterns and confusing drawings that seemingly have no significance. Although these are just a few characteristics, they can help you in finding a book that suits your interests.

Another indicator that may tell of the quality of a book is the presence of teasers, short blurbs found on the front and back covers of many paperback books. These blurbs function in making the book sound more appealing or worth reading and are written by the publisher. An example of a typical teaser is: "Number one-best-seller," written in black letters above the title. Because these are not written by book reviewers or critics, teasers are not always completely accurate in what they claim. If there are a whole lot of teasers on a cover, that is a pretty good sign that the book is of poor quality. Well written literature will usually have only one or two teasers which do not exaggerate the characteristics of the book.

However, well written literature may have many book reviews, which can easily be confused with teasers. Book reviews look much like teasers in that they tell how good the book is, but they are written by critics and are actual comments about the book. There are two ways book reviews are presented. The first way is the most credible and is written as a complete statement. "A dazzling feat of imagination," or, "Read this book if you read no other," or, "You can't put it down after you read the first page," are some examples. The second type is written as only a word or phrase of the review. "Intriguing. . ., Imaginative . . .Beautifully written. . .Interesting." this type of review is not always reliable and accurate because in the case of some books, only key words are quoted from the critic so as to make the review sound good when it might have really been bad. For example, suppose a quoted review read: "It is intriguing to me why anyone would want to read this book." The review on the cover might say just "Intriguing." Also, book reviews are good indicators if they are written by well-known reviewers or newspapers. Reviews that are signed, "New York Times,' or "Chicago Tribune," are usually accurate. But, beware of such names as "San Gabriel Valley Tribune," or "El Paso Times."

The last two indicators that can be used are the publisher and the reprinting information which can be found on one of the interior pages of the cover material. The publisher is a pretty good indicator because it is quick and easy to use. If the publisher's name is well-known, such as Dell, Random House, or Doubleday, the book possibly is of good quality. Otherwise, you should watch out for unknown publishers because this means the book may have been turned down by the major publishing companies.

Finally, the number of re-printings can serve as an excellent source for finding out how popular a book is and whether it has been read by many people. If there are more than three reprinting dates, chances are good that the book is of high quality.

Although there are many kinds of books on the shelves today, it can be determined that there are certain indicators in the cover material of a book that could tell you whether the book might be of interest to you. By examining a few of these indicators and what they mean, you can better understand how to find a book that suits you.

EXERCISE #5

Paper # 1

Cultural Perpetuators

Of all the cultures that have existed over the past three thousand years, only a select few have been able to endure for a long period of time. It is the stability of these cultures that has allowed them to prevail despite the constantly changing ideals of people. This condition of stability is present because the values that are most important to, or characteristic of a culture are not changed but passed on from generation to generation. In order for these values to be passed on, however, there must be institutions which function in perpetuating them. In America for instance, many cultural values are transmitted generationally through perpetuators such as schools, families, and children's toys.

School is an institution which almost every child attends and is, therefore, an effective perpetuator of those values which apply in a social environment. It is in the schools that children are taught such basic values as punctuality and recognition for performance.

The value of punctuality is highly stressed in the school environment. Children are taught that being on time is important and necessary. Although not prominent in most grade schools, the use of tardy bells in junior and senior high schools is commonplace. In fact, if the student has not developed the value of punctuality by the time he is in senior high school, he is punished in some way. Students who are late more than the allowed number of times are often referred to the principal's office or sent home with notices to their parents. In some cases, a student may actually lose credit for a level simply because he has not accepted a value. The majority of students accept punctuality as a value and become accustomed to what society expects from them.

Another value that is perpetuated in school is recognition for performance. This value basically says that if a student does something well, he is rewarded for it. The grading system found in almost every junior and senior high school demonstrates how widespread is this value. Based on the first five or six letters of the alphabet, the system allows students to receive a letter which has a specific merit or worth. Students who do well in school subjects receive letters closest to the beginning of the alphabet. Those who do exceptional work become members of the honor roll, a list of students who perform well. In elementary schools, where the alphabetic grading system is not as common, other symbols of recognition are used. Such symbols as gold stars, apples and smiling faces are often attached to the children's homework papers, tests or even to their foreheads so that every one will know they did well and have been rewarded.

One of the many important values a family exhibits is togetherness. Many adults remember this value best when they think back to their younger days. Whether it was joining Grandpa and Grandma for dinner on Sunday, going on a picnic with cousins, or taking a drive through the countryside on a nice Saturday afternoon with Mom and Dad, the attitude of togetherness was present.

It is through such activities that this value is passed on to children. A father may perpetuate the value of togetherness by taking his son fishing every Saturday morning. When the child gets older and has a family of his own, it is likely that he will do things with his children. Thus the value is perpetuated.

Responsibility is passed along in a similar manner. When most people think of responsibility, they think of several other values which are closely related. Values such as reliability, dependability, and trustworthiness are all commonly thought of as aspects of responsibility. Children are taught to tell the truth and honor their commitments, to help relatives or friends in need and to assume duties that must be performed, such as chores around the house. Responsibility is passed on through example, that is, the parents exhibit the value and the children in turn develop it. It is often the parents' job to point out when the children are lacking in responsibility and show them how to improve themselves.

The third cultural perpetuator, children's toys, is probably the second most influential in a young child's life. Since toys play a major role in how a child grows, it is obvious that values such as aggression and social status in relation to personal possessions are passed on through them. Aggression is a value which is evident in many toys for young boys. Almost every boy owns or has owned a toy gun, tank, knife or army doll, all of which perpetuate aggression. Parents buy these toys and are thereby passing along the value. It is quite common to see a group of boys playing cops and robbers or cowboys and Indian, games in which they actually pretend to kill each other. It is through these mock wars that many children develop their aggression value.

Finally, the value of social status in relation to personal possessions can also be found in children's toys. Actually, it is not found in any specific toy but in the number and quality of toys. For instance, a child who has many new, extravagant toys may feel that he is better or more important than the child with only a few, old warn-out toys. When these children are older, it is possible the children who had the better toys will have two cars, a big house, and expensive furniture, whereas the other children might have used cars, small houses and modest furnishings. Each child might develop the same value differently. The first child's value said it was important to have many expensive objects in order to be a worthy person. The other children might have been taught that the number of objects a person owns is not necessarily indicative of his worth.

Since it is essential to pass along certain values for the continued existence of our culture, it can be observed that through the use of institutions like school, churches and families, values are perpetuated effectively. By examining this process, it is hoped that one will better understand just how important the continued preservation of our values really is.

You notice that, even though the previous paper is well structured, this student didn't follow some of the directions very well. There are few examples and they were not given detail, and there were no pictures from books or toy catalogs. Below is a paper of another student who chose not to be so positive about middle level American values. You will notice that the writing is much more sophisticated.

Paper # 2

Perpetuation of Values

For any group of people to be called a society, a set of values must be established and perpetuated through successive generations. If this were not accomplished, the society would most likely fall apart, as each new generation would set up its own value system. Middle-level Americans may list their values as truth, justice and peace, but their actions rarely reflect these ideals. For this reason, the only way to effectively examine the true values of middle level society is to examine the actions of this group. In the middle level, the process of passing on values is practiced extensively, not only personally from generation to generation, but also through institutions. Because of this, each generation might be justified in saying that we have to live in a world that others make. Some of the values that are important to middle level Americans are violence, physical fitness, and sexism, which are perpetuated by children's toys, books and television.

One value that is very apparent in middle level society is violence, which is perpetuated by toys. One of the most violent popular toys is the GI Joe doll, a figure of a young muscular man dressed in full combat gear with knife, machine-gun, and grenade belt.

Displayed here a picture of GI Joe from a *Sears Christmas Catalogue*.

GI Joe has been popular for decades, and though his physical characteristics have changed, the value of violence behind the doll has not. Children still enjoy finding new and different ways to kill the "enemy."

The object of killing or destroying other things is also central in such toys as the Go-Bots Convertible Laser Gun and Cosmic Attack Cruiser, the Voltron Battle Riser, and the Wind Rider Assault Lander. Kids can wage war between their favorite heroes and villains with the Castle Greyskull Playset which includes Battle Cat, Battle Ram, Attack-Trak and Bashasaurus.

Picture here of "Voltron Battle Riser," *Sears Christmas Catalogue*.

They can even attack their friends and neighbors with the Omega Force Fantasy Rifle. It is obvious that these toys' main purpose is to promote violence.

Another institution that serves to pass on the value of violence is children's books. For centuries, stories that depict violent acts have been very popular with children and readily accepted by parents as suitable reading material. Such classic fairy tales as "Little Red Riding Hood," in which an old woman is eaten by a wolf, and "Hansel and Gretel" which ends with two children gleefully pushing a woman into an oven to her death, have very violent situations, but have never been considered objectionable by most middle level Americans.

More modern children's books also support violence as a value. The "He-Man" and "Masters of the Universe" series is the continuing story of the fight between He-Man and Friends against the evil villains of the universe. The characters in these books use knives, swords, laser guns, destructive dinosaurs and robots, and many other weapons to conquer each other. The only action is the killing or destroying of the enemy.

Television is also a perpetuator of violence for middle level America. Prime time programs such a "A Team" are targeted to the pre-teen audience, shown early enough in the evening to reach most children, and use violence as the main problem-solving technique. Car crashes, explosions, and killings are very common in these shows and often seen as real by the young viewer rather than as special effects.

A less realistic, but equally important type of television violence is the cartoon, a TV staple for millions of American children. Cartoons such as the "Bugs Bunny" the "Road Runner Hour" and "Dungeons and Dragons" are often very violent, with characters falling off of cliffs, being hit by trains, and being attacked by monsters.

The difference between these and live action programs, besides the obvious, is that in cartoons, the victims of violence usually end up no worse for their ordeals. This makes the violence seem less severe and easier for children to accept and incorporate into their own developing value systems.

Physical fitness is an American middle level value that has become very important. One of the perpetuators of this value is children's toys, a wide variety of which exhibit the qualities of physical fitness. For example, no Barbie or Ken doll, or any other doll for that matter, is overweight. Male dolls are always muscular and in perfect shape, and female dolls have slim waists, small hips and perfect figures. They are formed to the specifications of the physically perfect human.

Children are now being pushed at an early age to begin exercising and participating in sports to get in shape. Recently put on the market is an "Ultimate Workout Set" by Hasbro, which is designed for pre-teen girls. It includes dumbbells, a jump rope, an exercise mat, and a logbook to record workout times and techniques. The box reads that it is designed for ages five and up, even though there is no valid medical reason for any five year old to begin a rigorous exercise program as prescribed by this "toy."

Picture of "Ultimate Workout" Set, *Sears Christmas Catalog.*

Physical fitness is also stressed in children's books. Many children's stories in some way emphasize the value of physical fitness. Almost always, the main character of a story is in good physical condition, as are his family and friends. Often this character participates in athletics. If an antagonist is involved, he is often portrayed as overweight and a heavy eater, associating for the young reader "bad" with "out of shape."

There are also a number of children's exercise program books, such as *Mousiecise* by Walt Disney Productions, which comes with a cassette tape to play during the workout session. It takes kids through a series of aerobic style exercises toned down to children's abilities.

Picture of "Mousercise," *Sears Christmas Catalog.*

Television is another major perpetuator of physical fitness in America. Many different television programs, including cartoons, portray heroes as large muscular men capable of great feats of strength and endurance. Television women, too, are nearly always in good shape and well proportioned according to today's standards. Athletic competition, weight lifting, and other forms of exercise are often family activities in many programs aimed at children, such as "The Cosby Show" and "Family Ties."

Television also glorifies several sports figures with extensive coverage of athletic events such as football and baseball. Because many children idolize these sportsmen and women, they strive to be as much like them as possible, including the desire to be physically fit.

Another important American middle level value is sexism, which is passed on by children's toys. Many toys tend to adhere to traditional male and female roles such as the female as mother and housewife and the male as breadwinner and family leader. Toy advertisements, like those for Cabbage Patch dolls, always show the girl playing with dolls and never the boy doing so. Boys are usually shown with toy tool sets, lawn mowers, and doctor sets. Girls are usually used to model nurse and cheerleader costumes and play with toy stoves and cooking utensils. In these cases, the sexist value is very apparent.

Picture of girl with toy stove and boy with doctor set, *Sears Catalog.*

Children's books also serve to perpetuate sexism. Traditional male/female roles, especially in less recent books, are strictly followed. Many contain the image of the helpless woman in trouble being saved by the strong, handsome hero. "Cinderella" and "Sleeping Beauty" both exhibit this sexist role portrayal, and there are very few children's books that break the stereotypic mold. Family situation stories, almost without fail, portray the father as a working man who "wears the pants in the family." He usually is the one who doles out punishment, mows the lawn, and makes house repairs. An example of this is *Rosa-too-Little* by Sue Felt. "Rosa's father came home from work and set his briefcase on the hall table. . . "

Household mothers, however, are usually non-working housewives who tend to children and housework. This also is seen in Felt's book: "Rosa. . .ran into the kitchen where her mother was preparing dinner."

Another perpetuator of the sexist values in America is television, and works in much the same way as it does in Children's books. The same gender roles are often used as they are in books. Television shows such as the "A Team" portray men as the strong heroes getting "damsels in distress" out of trouble. The main characters of "The Dukes of Hazard" are two young, muscular men who create havoc in their town. They have a female cousin in her early twenties who wears skimpy clothes and constantly gets kidnaped by the "bad guys" and then must be saved by her cousins. Sexist attitudes such as these are seen in many television programs watched by middle level children.

Middle level Americans hold many values that have been given to them by earlier generations, and they continue to pass these values on using several perpetuating techniques. When examined, this process can very easily be seen.

Paper # 1

Role Model Changes Reflect Change in Children's Values

Throughout the centuries parents have passed their beliefs on to their children. Many of these beliefs represent values and are based on what they consider good and bad. Parents demonstrate their values to their children by spending time, money, and energy on the things that they care about. For instance, a child knows his parents care about him if they do things with him and take care of him, buying the things that he needs. Saying "I love you" and showing that love are two different things. Values are beliefs that are acted upon. Some of the values that the children of this generation are learning differ from those that their ancestors taught their children. Both television shows and children's literature from the last decade demonstrate changing values in the role of women in society.

Prior to nineteen seventy most children were taught that the role of the American woman was primarily in the home. The television shows that were broadcast and the books published during this era portray this value to children.

Family shows such as *Mr. Ed, Ozzie and Harriet, Dennis the Menace, and Leave it to Beaver,* all had mothers who were housewives. Viewers saw them dusting, vacuuming, ironing, making beds, and cooking meals. They always had supper ready for their families, had freshly baked pies and cakes awaiting consumption, and had cookies and milk for their children after school. They talked of going to P.T.A meetings, went shopping, and took turns having lady's circle meetings at their homes. They did everything that mothers do or were supposed to do, please their husbands, discipline their children, and gossip with their friends. Viewers saw them as happy housewives and children grew up dreaming of the ideal home. Girls dreamt of getting married and having children and boys grew up planning to find wives and support families.

Children's books like *The Happy Hollisters* and *The Bobbsy Twins on a Houseboat* by Laura Lee Hope, and Lois Lenskir's *Papa Small* all portray women as housewives. The first page of West's mystery shows mom pulling cookies out of the oven and helping Sue read a telegram. Many of these books tell of the day to day experiences of the children with their mothers in the background. The mothers are described cooking meals, cleaning house, doing laundry, mending, ironing, gardening, and baking. As housewives they work hard for their families and are always there for their children. The children rely on their mothers. They ask them how to do things hoping they will be able to solve their problems. Very few books with settings before nineteen-seventy show mothers that work outside the home because during this time period most women were housewives.

In nineteen-seventy the American economy slipped into a recession. One of the factors that contributed to this was the rise in the price of oil that the United States bought from Arabia; it went from three to forty-two dollars a barrel virtually overnight. During this same time, Japan had found a way to produce goods, especially automobiles, with little labor cost.

Since Japanese products were cheaper, Americans began to import far more than they exported. This helped boost the Japanese economy. However, because of the decrease in demand for American cars, thousands of men were laid off from their jobs in the automobile and steel industries. Many times their take-home pay was cut as they found jobs wherever they could to support their families. Just as Rosie the Riveter had rescued America and her family during World War Two, women began seeking employment to help support their families after their husbands income cuts. Even after the recession, women continued to work outside the home. Many times the money they made was a needed part of the family income, or it bought luxury items and funded vacations. Some married women managed to raise children and continue their careers. Other women who work are single parents and sole supporters of their children. Whatever the case, children have been taught different values about the role of American women in the last decade. Children's books and television shows help to shape and portray the new values that their parents have taught them.

Eleanor Claimer's children's book, *My Mother is the Smartest Woman in the World*, portrays the changes in values children have learned about women. Kathleen believes her mother is the smartest woman in town. After the mayor visits her school, she knows her mother can do a better job than he is doing. Kathleen's help with the campaign shows she wouldn't mind having her mother work and, in the end when her mother does become mayor, she is happy. Many children like Kathleen know their mothers are intelligent and believe they should work. Other children look to their mothers as the breadwinners because their parents are divorced. Laugh, in Beverly Clear's book, *Dr. Mr. Hence*, Mary, in *A Private Matter* by Kathryn Ewing and Gael and her brother, in Lean Paris's book, *Mom is Single* all live with their divorced mothers and accept their roles as supporters. Many children see working mothers as perfectly normal, feel their mothers should be able to work, and accept the added responsibilities so that they can work.

A great majority of the family shows that have been broadcast throughout the last decade show families with dual incomes. In *Raisin, The Cosby Show, ALF, Growing Pains*, and the ever classic *Family Ties*, both parents work. Although these television series show both parents working, they also show both of them spending time with their children. The parents seem to maintain a balance between work and family and share the responsibility of caring for the children. Beth in *Who's the Boss* and *Kate and Allie* role-play divorced family situations where the mothers work and bring up the children. On all the television shows with working mothers, the children accept their mother's roles and share household responsibilities so that their mothers can work.

Children are being taught that working women, especially mothers with jobs outside the home, are a part of life. As they read and watch television, these values are reinforced. Many of our ancestors would be shocked at the changes in the roles of women. Although it must be said that the history of the last decade has contributed to these changes.

The second student's writing for this exercise: (Not nearly as good a feel for the language.) Notice that this writer goes on and on and on long after the point has been made.

Paper # 2

Role Models

Young people, for as long as anyone can remember, have been looking for heroes or people to be role models. Usually they are people who are admired and looked up to. Long ago the president of our country and other political officers were often selected for role models. But these people are no longer respected in the ways they used to be. As time went on, inventors, scientists, and doctors were admired greatly for their knowledge and skills. Children even looked up to their parents as possible role models. It is sorry to say that most of these role models are pushed aside today and others have taken their places. Television has had a great deal to do with this. It presents people with different ideas of who their role models should be. Now many children and also some adults look up to sports heroes and other such people as their role models. Most often we adopt role models who have certain abilities in which we lack skill and that makes it all the more reason to admire them. Role models teach us about the world. There are models who show us the good side and some the bad side. But either way, we learn from them. The good role models teach us about love, unity, and the value of life, while bad role models show us drugs, violence, and killing. We need role models to help us understand about the world and the people in it. Television provides us with suitable role models who cast good influences on the adults of tomorrow. The qualities of the characters in the show *Family Ties* that enable them to be suitable role models are that Elise Keaton is organized, Stephen Keaton is caring, Alex is ambitious, Mallory is realistic, and Jennifer is accepting.

On the television series *Family Ties*, Elise Keaton has all of the qualities needed to present to the public an idea of what a suitable role model could be like. But the quality that most contributes to the fact that she is a good role model is that she is organized. She plays the role of the mother of four, wife, and working woman who through all of her activities still manages to maintain an organized household, care for her family, and continues to reach her goal of being a great architect.

An asset to the television screen, she goes on to prove that the woman of the eighties does not have to be confined only to housework and womanly duties. Loaded down with responsibilities to her work and her family, she continues to make a place for herself in the outside world. Since she is her own person, she tries to help her children become individuals and to make each of them feel unique. When they have troubles or are feeling insecure, more often than not they will turn to her for guidance and support. Although her schedule is usually hectic, she doesn't say, "I'm too busy," or, "Can't it wait until later?" she helps them in any way she knows how to. Small problems sometimes arise like the time Mallory messes up the hem on Jennifer's dress, as well as bigger ones such as when the new baby arrives and

Jennifer feels jealous and insecure, so she rebels against her parents.

But no matter what size the problem is, Elise Keaton is always there to lend her advice and understanding. Even her children's personal problems are brought to her attention. When Mallory is at the point in a relationship when she doesn't know how much farther it should go, she turns to her mother for advice.

Elise's children are not afraid to come to her with any problems they might have. She is a sympathetic listener and is able to give them good advice. Elise often brings her work home with her but she doesn't let it interfere with her responsibilities to her family. She organizes her time wisely so not only can she get her work finished but also spend time with her family. Her character role is a good example of what the modern woman should be like.

The character role of the father is played by Stephen Keaton, whose main attribute that enables him to be an appropriate role model is that he is caring. He is the kind of person who puts his family first. He actually cares about what his children become and he's not one to let them run wild. If a member of the family has a problem, he likes to talk it over with them and try to help in any way possible.

Besides being a caring father, he's also a very caring husband. He worries whether his wife works too hard or is too tired after taking care of Andrew, who has just entered pre-school. To him, his wife and kids deserve the best and he doesn't want to ever see them get hurt. A situation in the show when he fully realizes how much his family really means to him is when he is offered a promotion which requires a lot of traveling. He goes on a business trip for the weekend and starts talking about his family and that is when the loneliness overcomes him. Thoughts go through his mind about whether he's being a good husband or raising his kids right because he hasn't been around them much lately to help them with their problems or just talk to them. That is when he decides that the promotion is not worth being apart from his family constantly. He returns to his old job and apologizes to his family for neglecting them.

There is also a circumstance in one of the shows when Stephen could have gotten involved with a woman who was in love with him but he told her that he cared too much about his wife to get involved with her. His caring is not only limited to his family. Skippy, their neighbor, who is often ridiculed, and Stephen's fellow workers are others who earn a special place in his heart.

Besides caring about people he also cares about world events. He is against war and the use of weapons and he cares deeply about the shape the country is in. All of these qualities plus more give him the status of being a very good role model.

Alex is ambitious, a characteristic he is well-known for and that helps to make him a good role model on the show. He is more or less the most popular character in this series. Not only is he ambitious but he is funny too. Alex and his sense of humor are the main reasons the show is so popular. He sets his goals and chases after them like a house of fire. When he wants something bad enough and tries hard for it, chances are he'll get it. When Alex sets his mind on something, he sticks with it. That's how a person has to be to reach his goals. In more than one way the word *ambitious* describes him. Alex wants to be a straight "A" student so he sets that goal and works really hard to achieve it, and he does. He's very smart and so all he has to do is apply himself to do well. Another show of ambitiousness refers to the time

Ellen, the girl he loves, leaves to marry a different guy and Alex wants to let her know how he feels about her, so he drives a couple of hundred miles to the railroad station. By luck she decides not to board the train and they come to the conclusion that they love each other. Alex is also very eager to make money. He thinks he is a born businessman and will someday be very successful. With this in mind, he rents a room of their house to a family when his parents are away and one thing leads to another and before he knows it they have a house full of people. His dream of making a lot of money by using their house as a hotel for the weekend quickly dissolves when his parents come home early and find all the people and a kangaroo in their living room. Sometimes being ambitious is a good trait, but in this case it got him into a scrape. Alex is ambitious and knows what he wants out of life but is unwilling to hurt others who stand in the way of his goals. That combination makes him an excellent role model.

Mallory, the Keaton's oldest daughter, is realistic, a trait which helps her cope with the pressures of the world around her. For instance, Alex is much smarter than Mallory and she realizes this. She doesn't try to be better or smarter than him because she knows that she couldn't be. In this way she is being realistic.

There is an episode on the show when Mallory tells Alex that she could never be as smart as him or attend a college as good as the one he attends because her grades would never live up to the expectations needed to enter a reputable college. She admits her faults and goes on with life doing the best she can do. Although it sometimes seems unlikely, she knows what she wants out of life and strives for it with much vigor and enthusiasm. When the show first aired Mallory seemed like someone who only cared about shopping, boys, and other such trivial things. But she has now matured and acknowledges the value of life and all the treasures it holds. She fully understands what life has in store for her and all of the opportunities that are available. Running a small business is something that Mallory experiments with in the show. She chooses something within her limits and that she can make a success: a clothes store. Her career choices are based on the abilities she has and where her interests lie. Mallory is definitely a suitable role model because she is realistic in her views and accepts herself for who she really is.

Jennifer is the youngest daughter in the family and has the disposition of being very accepting. She is a far different person from either her older brother or sister. Sometimes the middle child has the tendency to look up to older brothers and sisters and try to follow in their footsteps. But Jennifer is so unlike both Alex and Mallory that she has to accept the fact that she is her own person and mold her own personality. She takes all this in stride and does a good job in being herself. For a while on the show she is a tomboy. She plays sports and has many friends that are boys. Many of them treat her just like one of the guys because of her tomboyish ways, but she is accepting throughout this period of time. Jennifer and Mallory are as different as night and day. Mallory enjoys shopping and boys while through her tomboyish period, Jennifer is only interested in sports and any physical activity. All through this time Jennifer understands that she and Mallory have different interests and cannot share them for a while. At first this is difficult for her to accept because it is natural for sisters to do things together, but she soon realizes that they are still close even if their interests aren't the same. Later in the series their mother, Elise, gives birth to a baby boy and all of their lives are

82

changed although at the time it seems that Jennifer is the one who undergoes the most change. Up until the baby is born, Jennifer is the baby of the family and is given a lot of attention. But that all changes very quickly. The baby is the center of attention and Jennifer feels rejected and rebels against her family. This is an example when at first she doesn't accept something but slowly learns to. After her feelings of jealousy are put to rest, she begins to really enjoy the new baby and realizes that her place in the family has not been taken away from her. All of these situations help contribute to the fact that Jennifer is an accepting person and therefore a good role model.

The role models on television today are suitable for providing good influences on children. In the television series *Family Ties*, the features of the main characters that allow them to be suitable role models are that else Keaton is organized, Stephen Keaton is caring, Alex is ambitious, Mallory is realistic, and Jennifer is accepting. The traits of the characters on *Family Ties* enable them to be good role models to the children who view the show on television. By now the reader should have decided that today's television role models are suitable and afford good influences on children.

You will recognize that that writer has her mind made up about her subject and understands the ideas of support in exposition. There are many problems with this paper, and I'm sure you can spot them.

EXERCISE #7

The Discriminative Ability

The ability to discriminate plays an extremely important role in how we live our lives, but it is probably one of the most complicated and misunderstood concepts we have. The common definition of discrimination, the process by which we consciously accept or reject something, is not really correct. The standard definition is, the process by which we differentiate between choices by analyzing the options by comparison and contrast. The fact that most people accept the incorrect definition demonstrates why, throughout history, man has ignored his discriminative abilities.

When our past is scrutinized, it is easy to recognize that generally we did not use our discriminatory skills very well. An example is that our world is very badly polluted. If we had discriminated years ago when we first noticed what was happening, if we had looked at all of the pros and cons of the causes of pollution and decided which was more important; to have large factories that spill vast amounts of pollutants into the environment, killing much of the plant and animal life and altering the ecology or to find some alternative manufacturing techniques that would limit the amount of pollution and waste, our world would not be in its present condition.

Had we gone through the discriminatory process and made a reasonable decision before we bombed Hiroshima, we would have possibly come up with an alternative. Instead, we simply decided that what we wanted was to win the war and we determined the Japanese were bad people. We never analyzed the situation logically.

Since the discriminatory process is such an integral part of life, it should be taught somewhere so that it could be understood and employed correctly. But, of the three places where learning takes place: school, home, and church, not one teaches how to discriminate. Our society seems to be content to leave the learning of this ability up to each individual. And the only way a person can learn to discriminate is by trial and error. History demonstrates, though that we don't do very well when it comes to this area. So here we have a "no win" situation in which we must make daily decisions based upon our discriminative ability and yet, this ability is not taught anywhere in our society. To show why this is so necessary and how complicated the discriminatory process is, the discrimination of a pen and a pencil was analyzed and the similarities and differences in regard to function, design, aesthetics, durability, cost, and material made from were recognized and recorded.

The discrimination of a White Brothers, Paper Mate ball point pen and a Faber Castell number two pencil, two relatively similar objects, is a very involved process. In regard to function, they are alike in that they are both used primarily for writing purposes. The pen, which writes in blue ink, is useful when a more permanent kind of writing is required. But, since the ink is not erasable, there is no efficient way of correcting mistakes. The pencil, however, has an eraser attached which allows modifications or deletions to be made. The eraser is the feature that makes the pencil more advantageous at times. Graphite is the material that is erasable and it is a shade of gray in color.

84

The design of the two objects is also very similar in most ways. Both are long, round, and slender. This area, which will be referred to as the body, functions as a holding area for the writing material (ie. ink, graphite). The pen is about six inches long, while the pencil, when new, is approximately eight inches long. Both are tapered to a point at the writing end. The pen is equipped with a cap, which functions in keeping the ink fresh. The pencil has an eraser which is attached by a metal band.

In the case of aesthetics, neither of the writing utensils is extremely beautiful. The pen has a shiny white body with the name and location of its manufacturer printed in black letters. The words, *Paper Mate* and *med. pt. U.S.A.* are written in capital letters, whereas "White Bros." is written as an artistic logo. The part of the pen which tapers toward the ball point is an aqua blue color, as is the cap. The whole pen has a smooth, streamlined appearance. The pencil is a school-bus yellow in color, with the words *Faber Castell* and *American* printed in black block letters. There is a black oval, approximately 6/16 inches long and 1/8 inch wide with a number two (2) inscribed in it towards the eraser end. The eraser is a reddish brown color and is clamped to the rest of the pencil with a shiny, silver metal band. The light brown wood is visible where the pencil is sharpened and it gives away to a dark gray graphite tip. The pencil's body is not completely round like the pen's body is. It is a hexagonal shape, with six sides equal in width.

An examination of durability is also a quality which demonstrates how these objects are similar and different. Both the pen and pencil are durable to a certain but different degree. It is possible to break the pen's body if enough force is exerted. The pencil's body requires about one-fifth the force to snap and it breaks much like a tree twig does. In terms of how long each lasts, the pen has the shorter life span because the ink is used up faster than the graphite of the pencil.

The fifth distinction, cost, shows no similarity. The pen costs, on the average, about eighteen cents, whereas the pencil's cost averages about seven cents.

Finally, the material that the two are made from is the most drastic difference. The pen is made of a plastic tube filled with ink and encased in a strong lightweight plastic body. The writing end has a small metal tip with a ball attached to the ink tube. The pencil, on the other hand, is composed of a tiny rod of graphite mixed with pipe clay and enclosed in a red cedar case. Other components include the rubber eraser and metal band which wraps around the eraser and holds the eraser in place.

An understanding of just how is difficult it is to discriminate carefully, as demonstrated by the complexity of the discrimination of two simple objects, shows how we might be more careful to take the time and really think things through carefully the next time we are faced with a decision.

85

Egocentric People

Human beings participating in exchanges of words tend to only enjoy the conversation if it accommodates their own interests. Most humans are egocentric and they enjoy conversing on their own level and subject. Therefore, most people enjoy verbal interactions in direct proportion to their own interests. In demonstration of the validity of this concept, examples of three conversations between the initiator/author and three teenagers have been transcribed including the teenagers' verbal and physical reinforcements toward the initiator/author. The conversations differ in aspect by the number of times the words *I* and *you* are used. In the first example *I* is used quite frequently and *you* not at all, whereas in the second example *I* and *you* are used equally as much. In the third example *I* is omitted from the initiator's speech and he uses only *you*.

The first conversation took place in the cafeteria of Niles High School during the lunch hour. The initiator had finished eating and walked over to sit by the subject who was also done eating. The initiator began to speak quite frankly about himself using the word *I* often and not using the word *you* at all. The initiator/author is designated by *A*, and the subject by *S*.

A: Hi! I just got done eating and I thought I might stop by and say hello. (The initiator sat down.) Boy, wasn't that food bad today? I really thought it stunk. I ate it anyway 'cause I was so hungry but it was really horrible.

S: (Nodding in agreement.) Yea, I thought so too. So, what have you been up to?

A: Well, until last week I was playing basketball and my team did really good this year. We were 15-2 and I had a lot of fun. I wish the season wasn't over because I'm really gonna' miss it.

S: I know how you feel, (Looking down at his plate and proceeding to stick his plastic fork into the styrofoam, making little holes in it as he was listening.)

A: I'm going to play baseball this spring. That starts in a couple of weeks.

S: Oh, that should be fun, (Stops playing with the fork and looks around the cafeteria as if searching for someone.) Well, I guess I'll be going. Bye.

During the entire conversation, the subject showed little interest in what the initiator was saying. Although there were some verbal reinforcements such as: *Oh, really?* and *Yea*, and *Uh huh*. The subject rarely met eye to eye with the initiator while he was talking. The subject also showed disinterest by playing with the fork and styrofoam plate.

The second conversation also took place in the cafeteria of Niles High School during the lunch hour. The initiator was sitting by the subject and they were both eating their lunches. In conversation two, the words *I* and *you* are used in equal number by the initiator. The conversation begins with the initiator asking the subject if he can be seated.

A: Can I sit down here?

S: Sure, (Sliding over her chair a little to allow room for the initiator to sit.)

A: How ya been?

S: Pretty good. How 'bout you?

A: I'm doing pretty good too. (Takes a bite of food and then begins to speak again.) So, what have you been up to?

S: Not a whole lot. I've been keeping busy with cheerleading, you know. We've only got a few games left so after that's over I don't know what I'll be doing. Your basketball team did really well this season didn't it? What was your record?

A: Ah, we were 15-2.

S: That's excellent, (Smiling and looking right at the initiator.) You guys are gonna' be real good when you are seniors, I bet.

A: I sure hope so. It's kind of hard to tell right now though.

S: Yea, you're probably right. (Has finished her lunch, gets up and carries her tray to the wastebasket.) I'll see you later.

A: Okay, bye.

During this conversation, the subject was obviously interested in what was being said. She smiled and showed facial expressions that were physical reinforcements.

The third example of conversation took place in the hallway of the math wing of the Niles High School after school. The initiator walked up to the subject who was standing by an open locker getting her books.

The initiator uses the word *you* frequently but *I* is not used at all.

A: Hi! How are ya?

S: Oh, just fine. How 'bout you?

A: Great! So, what have you been up to?

S: I'm in the musical right now. (Smiling.)

A: Oh, really? How's it shaping up this year?

S: It's coming along pretty well. It's a lot of fun, but it's also a lot of hard work. We've got a good cast and it should be a real good show. (Lots of animation and smiles.)

A: What is it?

S: *Annie Get Your Gun.*

A: Oh, that sounds familiar!

S: (Smiles) Yea, it's about Annie Oakley and the wild west and the *Buffalo Bill*

Show. It's a comedy-western I guess.

A: Hmm. . .Sounds like it's gonna be good. It looks like you got homework.

S: (Nods her head) Yea, I've got it in just about every level tonight.

A: Have fun. See ya later.

S: Bye. (She turns to close her locker)

During this conversation, the subject was very willing to talk about herself, and the initiator helped her along with the use of the word *you* and the elimination of the word *I* from his part of the conversation.

After examining these three conversations, it becomes obvious that the three subjects responded to the initiator's conversation with more enthusiasm when the word *I* was used less by the initiator. This would seem to support the idea that people really are most interested in themselves and things that have to do with themselves. It is obvious that if we want other people to enjoy talking to us we should not talk about ourselves.

The Success in Failures

Eugene Linden has addressed the subject of education in his latest essay, "Education," in *Affluence and Discontent*. The main thrust of Linden's essay is his claim that the American system is designed to produce failures. His subordinate idea is that the failures of this system are really successes.

It is somewhat understandable why Linden feels this way. Recently, a study was made at ACLU that showed over 40% of America's school children cannot read effectively, and more than half of the adult population is semiliterate. "Today, after the spending of billions of dollars toward primary and remedial reading programs and decades of effort to achieve literacy, these people simply cannot read," says Linden.

"They have failed the system," according to Richard Bowen, superintendent of the Buffalo, New York Community Schools. Linden claims, "Because there is no apparent opposition to literacy, what we can conclude from our failure to impart this basic skill is that it is not a basic skill. Although we may idealize universal literacy, perhaps it is not in the best interests of a consumer society to achieve it."

Gerald Drysdall, a well known voice in education as well as a general sales manager for the consumer Products Division of the Chrysler Corporation, agrees with Linden. "Maybe the failures of American education are necessary to the economy and the consumer society. We have 732 Mexican-Americans in our plants now, 84 % can't read, much less write. Yet, they belong to the union and are making good money. We couldn't function without them."

Cynthia McConnell, a social worker in Detroit, says, "Those people who have failed the system have not necessarily failed in life, they have succeeded in filling those jobs that are not filled by those persons who did succeed in the educational system."

Mrs. Annette Kirk, member of the National committee on Excellence in Education, expressed her concern for the illiterate in the American education system this way: "Those persons who make it through the required educational programs, and are still illiterate, are forced to seek those jobs at lower income levels compared to those persons who are literate and go on to higher education."

One of Linden's supportive ideas is that the way a student reacts to and accomplishes in the structure of the educational system determines that student's role in future consumer life. He says that, "A great preponderance of the. . .innovators are often either academic failures or academically indifferent." This may be true, but a large number of these innovators are academic successes, also. Linden himself gives the example of Edwin Land, a brilliant Harvard graduate who started Polaroid. This claim seems to be in conflict with a later statement, "Those who fail to master the forms and subject matter are the nation's labor force." He later goes on to explain that these academic failures are the buyers and subjects of advertisers. Linden seem to be confusing himself with his words.

Linden has tried to create an important and controversial article, but has not succeeded. Behind the intellectual sounding language is a confused and confusing piece of unsupported speculation which has little or no value for me in my deciding a position on this question.

EXERCISE #10

Paper 1 of exercise #10

Biasing

This survey was conducted at Niles Senior High School, Niles, Michigan. It comprises the responses of thirty students selected as a cross-section sample of the student body. The questions were not asked in the order they are presented here, but were mixed up in order to hide the nature of the biasing. But, for this report, the unbiased and biased questions are here grouped together. In each group of two questions, the first one is the bias-free question and the second one is the same question but it has been biased to influence the respondents answers.

Questions 5 & 6, 7 & 8, and 9 & 10 are cross-negative responses. For instance, in questions 5 & 6 the 17 "Yes" responses decrease to 2 responses of the same nature even though the responses are "No" responses.

(bias-free question)
1. Do you feel the death penalty is a fair punishment for someone who has committed murder?

    Yes 22   No 8

(biased question)
2. Do you think that all of the convicted murderers who are currently serving prison sentences should be put to death as punishment for their actions?

    Yes 10   No 20

3. Do you believe the United States is right by countering the Soviet's nuclear arms build-up with our own mass production of nuclear weapons?

    Yes 19   No 11

4. Do you feel that the nuclear arms race between the U.S. and the Soviet Union is justified even though the two nations currently possess enough nuclear warheads to completely destroy our world many times over?

    Yes 12   No 18

5. Is the right to obtain a divorce a positive aspect of our culture?

    Yes 17   No 13

6. Do you feel divorce is a contributing factor to the breakdown of our society's family structure as well as the emotional and physical strains experienced by children whose parents are divorced?

    Yes 28   No 2

7. Is it your opinion that abortion is right because it is an effective method of dealing with unwanted pregnancy?

    Yes 17   No 13

8. Do all human beings have the right to life from the time of conception?

    Yes 21   No 9

9. Do you believe nuclear energy should be strongly considered as an energy resource of the future?

Yes 20   No 10

10. Is it your opinion that nuclear power plant incidents, such as the one at Three Mile Island, demonstrate that nuclear energy is dangerously unsafe and should not be considered as an alternative energy resource?

Yes 18   No 12

This student did a fine job even though there was a decrease of 40% in positive response.

Paper #2 of exercise #10

Genetic Research

Ever since James Watson and Robert Crick discovered the DNA structure in 1962, man has been fascinated by the field of genetic research. Their discovery opened the door for many incredible scientific breakthroughs. Neither Watson or Crick probably ever realized what sort of an impact their efforts in genetic study would have on the present and future ways of life. For instance, the concept of cloning is currently being explored and scientists are gaining a better understanding of the mechanics involved in the procedure. It may actually be possible, within a few years, to replicate a human being who would possess exactly the same characteristics as the original. The ability to "read genes" allows genetic counselors to determine if the offspring of two people could have any serious mental or physical deficiency or inherited diseases. Also, genetic engineering, which involves the manipulation of genes to produce an individual with certain desired traits, is a rapidly advancing area of genetic research.

However, some people feel that the knowledge scientists are gaining in genetic research is "dangerous knowledge." Much like the invention of the atomic bomb, genetic research is thought by some, to have the possibility of going too far. History demonstrates that when man is introduced to new knowledge, he almost always ends up putting the knowledge to work. And, in many cases he goes too far and exploits the knowledge.

Because areas of genetic research such as cloning, genetic counseling, and genetic engineering are becoming more and more of a reality, it is likely that at some time, in the not too distant future, we will be asked to state our opinions or vote on such issues. For analytical purposes, this examination was assembled containing a fair presentation of the arguments for and against genetic research, which were broken down into areas of morality and danger.

Some of the most recent advances in genetic research have been in genetic counseling. Genetic counseling is a developing medical procedure which helps couples make decisions about child bearing based on knowledge that in most cases was unobtainable a few years ago. One of the most important things about genetic counseling is that a couple may decide against marriage after they have been counseled, for knowing their offspring would have a good chance of being ugly or stupid, would surely force them to reconsider their marital plans. Since it is also possible to determine the sex of the child soon after conception, is would be easy to abort the child if it was not of the wanted sex. Also, the abortion rate would probably show a decrease because children would not be given a chance to live in the first place. There would be no need to kill them.

Fortunately, there is almost no danger to the mother in any of the previously discussed counseling tests, but the negative effects experienced by the baby are not yet full recognized. Genetic counseling, although not widely practiced today, might possibly become commonplace or even required by law in the future.

Another area of genetic research, cloning, has not yet been experimented enough with to be practiced on humans but is likely to be practiced within the next fifty years at the current rate of scientific advance. The cloning procedure involves taking a cell from an individual and growing an exact replica in a surrogate mother. The cell can be of any type: skin, internal organ, fingernail, etc., because all of the cells of an individual contain the exact same chromosomes, traits, and genes. Even though many people feel cloning goes against the Christian views of morality, and would have a drastically detrimental effect on our society, it does have its advantages. For example, famous or important people such as Einstein, Michelangelo, or Adolph Hitler could all be cloned, preserving their unique characteristics. It is impossible, however, to determine the effects such events would have on the world. Cloning could also ease the pain that a family experiences when a relative is killed or dies. If a child were to be killed, the family could have one of the child's genes dissected and a replica child could be made. Although the child would not be the original, he would be so close to the original it would be virtually impossible to tell he was actually an impostor. So, it can be clearly seen that cloning would definitely change the way we live and die.

A third area of genetic research, genetic engineering, is closely related to cloning. It however, does not involve the replication of an entire individual but only desired traits. For example, if a couple were to want to have their child grow up to be a criminal genius, they could have their chromosomes analyzed by a specialist who would determine what chromosomes would have to be destroyed and then produce the desired chromosomes which would be attached when the egg and sperm cell unite. The child would grow like any normal child but he would possess the characteristics of a criminal genius. Fully any trait could be instilled in a child. However, the possibility of mutant genes developing is much greater in the genetic engineering procedure. In essence, the natural child who would have developed without the intervention of a genetic engineer would be killed and replaced by the new child. The genetic engineering field is still very much untested and based mostly on theory.

Looking at the negative side of genetic research, one can see there are as many drawbacks as there are advantages. For instance, if cloning were to be practiced with humans, the effects that might occur could possibly be devastating to the people of our world. Given time, scientists would probably keep upgrading their abilities and our society would gradually begin to resemble a somewhat utopian civilization. Such a society would have virtually no chance of existence, however, because there are always those individuals who are inferior or imperfect and the end result would be a majority of people flung into an unstable lower level. One could visualize a picture of an inhuman, almost machine-like civilization in which all inhabitants would look, act, and think the same. Cloning would completely destroy the uniqueness of individuals and it is feasible that a Hitler-like master race could be created. Even worse, an evil person such as Hitler himself could be cloned and rise to power. Aside from the dangerous aspects, cloning is considered by many to be, simply, a moral wrong. Many people have the opinion, "If God had wanted duplicates of people made, He would have created a twin for every human being on Earth." Although at first the prospects that are presented by cloning appear to be positive and exciting, after further examination, this procedure seems to weigh more heavily as a detrimental aspect of our future.

Another bleak result that could come about if genetic research is explored and studied to its fullest extent is that the knowledge gained could fall into the wrong hands and be used against the mass of people. Any large company could "set up shop" in a small foreign country and practice unsafe experiments. If such a company were to have access to the most recent genetic research data, it could illegally conduct unregulated experiments and create an organism or mutant of a dangerous nature. Most scientists agree that any accident would affect other parts of the globe. It is quite frightening to realize how much power an individual or group of individuals would have if he or they were to possess a mutant microbe that could cause a deadly disease capable of wiping out the human race. It would be much the same as terrorists having a hydrogen bomb capable of blowing up the world. Unless genetic research is restricted and carefully regulated, the knowledge gained could lead to a catastrophic disaster.

If cloning, genetic counseling, and genetic engineering were to become standard procedure, our current family structure would be altered drastically.

In many cases, family members would not feel the love for each other that is present in today's society. There would be a deterioration of the close-knit family life that most people are used to. These scientific methods do not require the intimate emotional involvement that is required by today's society. A person could not enjoy the unique qualities of another. Our world would be an impersonal, cold, and lonely place to live.

Since genetic research is a field that is expanding at an extremely rapid rate, one would be wise to get acquainted with some of the arguments that are often used on the issue. By examining and better understanding some of the views that are presented on the issue of genetic research, it is hoped that one can form a personal opinion that is completely justified.

Paper #3 of exercise 10

The Biased Ability

Usually, when two people disagree over their opinions on an issue, they both feel that they are correct and that their positions are justified despite their base difference in views. Often, when the arguments for and against are presented, one person is able to make the other reconsider his opinion or change his mind. The ability to influence a person's belief is a valuable skill, and is utilized in many areas of our society. For instance, many of the surveys that are conducted by organizations to determine the public's opinions use questions that are worded in such a way so as to influence the responses. Also, many articles found in popular news and political magazines are composed in a similar manner, so that one side of an issue or subject is made to look better, more advantageous, or more attractive than the other. This method of influencing a position is called biasing.

The most important aspect of biasing is that it must be done so that it is unrecognizable to the reader. One who is experienced at writing biased statements can, on the ostensible level, appear to be fair by treating both sides of an issue equally, while in reality he may be influencing the reader toward one side or the other. For example, a person who is a strong advocate of nuclear energy might pick up a magazine and read an article on the positive and negative aspects of nuclear energy in the future. The article might appear to give both sides equal treatment, but the author could actually have biased it against nuclear energy. If the reader hadn't recognized the presence of the biasing technique by the time he finished the article, his opinion might be weakened or changed completely. The ability to bias statements is relatively easy to learn to do. To demonstrate the simplicity of this technique, some of the mechanics used in biasing such as: number of arguments used, careful selection of words used, and short/long term memory, are described and examined as they were employed in an article and a survey.

The first technique requires subtleness and it is the most easily detected if done incorrectly. It involves the number of arguments for and against the issue. The side that the reader is to be influenced toward has one more argument than the other side has. However, since it is imperative that the reader think the issues are being presented fairly, the extra argument must be hidden or disguised so that it is not easily discovered.

The article which will be used as an example is titled "Genetic Research" and was written by this author. In the article, the pros and cons of genetic research are argued and there is one more argument against genetic research than there is for, because the author wanted the reader to be influenced against genetic research. The arguments for the issue include: the advantages of cloning, the positive aspects of genetic counseling, and the advantages of genetic engineering. Arguments against the issue include: the possible negative effects of cloning, dangers of genetic information falling into the wrong hands, the possible creation of a Hitler-like supreme race, and the ill-effects that our society would suffer if genetic research were to be continued. The two views which argue the negative aspects of cloning and the possible creation of a supreme race are combined so the reader won't notice the presence of an extra argument. That area of the article reads like this:

> . . .if cloning were to be practiced on humans, the effects that might occur could possible be devastating. One could visualize a picture of an inhuman, almost machine-like society in which all inhabitants look, act, and think the same. Cloning would completely destroy the uniqueness of individuals, and it is feasible that a Hitler-like master race would be created.

The second technique, use of words with known connotations, is probably the most effective in influencing the reader. It involves the employment of words which have a known positive or negative connotation for the intended readership. This method works because it gives the reader an impression about his reading. In the arguments for genetic research, negative words are used, whereas positive words are used in the arguments against. It is hoped that after the reader has finished the article, he will have a bad feeling about further genetic research and a good feeling about abandoning the field. Such statements as the following all exhibit the use of words that are designed in the paper to affect the reader in negative ways.

> One of the most important things about genetic counseling is that a couple may *decide against marriage* after they have been counseled, for knowing their offspring would have a good chance of being *ugly or stupid*, would surely *force* them to reconsider their marital plans.

> . . .and the abortion rate would decrease because the child would not be given a *chance to live* in the first place so there would be no need to *kill it*.

> . . .for example, famous or important people such as Einstein, Michaelanglo and *Hitler* could be cloned.   . . .if a child were to be *killed*, the family could have one of his genes dissected and a *replica* made. . .

This technique is also employed in the survey which is made up of ten questions concerning such current issues as: capital punishment, the nuclear arms race, divorce, abortion, and nuclear energy. In reality, however, the survey is composed of only five questions, asked in two different ways: biased and bias-free. Some of the questions contain words of positive or negative connotation.

> Is the *right to obtain* a divorce a *positive aspect* of our culture?

> Do you think that all of the *convicted murderers* . . should be *put to death* as *punishment* for their actions?

> Is it your opinion that abortion is an effective *method* of dealing with *unwanted* pregnancy?

The final biasing technique is short/long term memory use, and it applies only to the article. This technique involves simply the placement of the arguments in the article. Those arguments which support the side that the reader is to be influenced toward are placed after the arguments which support the other side. In the sample article, all of the arguments that support genetic research are placed first, while the arguments against the issue are placed afterward. This technique works, because the reader remembers best the things he has read most recently.

Almost all of these techniques are effective in the article and survey. Of the three people who read the article, two said their opinions of the issue of genetic research had been weakened. Both were in favor of its continued research before they read the article but weren't so sure of their positions afterwards. The survey, which was taken of a cross-section of students in a high school, shows how biasing a question could bring about a desired response. On the average, there was a decrease of fifty-three percent in the positive responses when the questions were biased.

Since biasing can be found in many areas of our society and is used, in some cases, to take advantage of the readers of it, it might be wise to gain a better understanding of how it works. By examining some of the basic techniques of biasing, one can realize that it is a relatively easy process to employ and that almost anyone can learn to do it effectively.

EXERCISE #11

The following paper was written by a high school senior as propaganda for the pro-choice view of the abortion question. Don't think that I want you to agree with this position; I included it because you should recognize some of the propaganda techniques that are in this piece that you've heard and read in recent months.

Abortion Not Wrong

Twelve years ago, the U.S. supreme Court ruled that abortion was legal until the moment of birth. It was a sound, well thought-out decision, one which has made this country a better place to live. But, there are those who feel this was a poor decision and that abortion should be outlawed completely. We, as rational, right-thinking Americans must wake up to this attempt to destroy our proud nation. Don't these anti-abortion supporters realize what outlawing abortion would do to this great country of ours?

Just look at one example, mental retardation. An estimated seventy-seven thousand babies were born last year with serious, permanent, mental deficiencies. These babies will grow up relying totally on us for everything. Many will be put into mental institutions (which are run and maintained with our money) and never live productive lives. They will make no positive contribution to society. On the contrary, they will be a heavy burden on it. A burden on us, our children, and our children's children. Those who are not institutionalized will be forced to live any way and anywhere they can. There are now between five hundred thousand and one million people, many of whom were born mentally deficient, living in the streets of our nation's cities. These people are a menace to our society! Without legal abortion, their numbers will multiply at an incredible rate and they will have the capability to overthrow our precious social structure. We will be living in a country which won't even remotely resemble the America that now exists. Those who wish to outlaw abortion surely must understand the inevitable results. Who do they persist in their crusade? Is It because they have made plans to make this nightmare a reality?

And let's consider the effects of unwanted childbirth. Obviously, if a mother doesn't want a child but is forced to have one against her will, she is not going to give that child the love and kindness that it needs. Sure, a life has been saved, but is the child better off now, being beaten and abused, shipped from orphanage to orphanage? Statistics clearly point out that seven of every ten federal crimes (rape, murder, armed robbery, etc.) are committed by people who were abused or sexually molested as children. Those against abortion must feel that child abuse isn't all that bad. Again, we end up with a society dominated by criminals and misfits. This doesn't have to be! Abortion provides an effective and painless method of eliminating the entire problem.

Do we want to be terrified to walk the streets of our fine cities? Do we want our children to grow up in an America dominated by criminals and social outcasts? Do we want to destroy everything our fathers and grandfathers have done to make America the land of the free and the home of the brave? Do we want to outlaw abortion? It is time we put an end to this threat.

The same student writing for paper #2 of exercise 11

The Techniques Behind Propaganda

Propaganda techniques, which appear in several communicative media, are commonly used to produce social actions or responses. Despite their frequent occurrences, these techniques are not consciously recognized by the majority of people, simply because most people don't understand what propaganda is or does. Propaganda is usually thought of as being ideas, facts or allegations spread deliberately to further some cause or to damage an opposing cause. Most Americans think of wartime when they hear this word, and the images of Hitler and his terrible deeds as depicted on anti-Nazi posters often pop into their minds. However, propaganda can vary a great deal in subtlety and it is the more subtle material with which we come most into contact. Regardless of its form, the mechanical aspects of propaganda can be exemplified in several techniques which are effective when employed correctly with respect to the subject matter. An examination of a serious propaganda pieces and a parody of propaganda was made in which some of the more obvious techniques were analyzed.

A common technique in propaganda writing, Implication of Co-interest, is successfully employed when the author suggests that the reader and he have similar interests, values, goals and desires. If the reader believes he and the author stand for the same things, he will be more likely to react positively to what the author tells him. In a recent letter to the editors of a newspaper the writer uses this technique:

> The picture you see is so violent you will not doubt that little girl felt pain as she throws her head back in a silent scream before being dismembered. It is a victim's point of view seen with your own eyes.
> Unless reasoned, intelligent pursuit of abortion violence is made by Americans soon, indifference will destroy our once great nation.

The technique also can be observed in the parody, "The Devil's Advocate."

> We have been warned about the international communist conspiracy corrupting our children.
> And what about the American capitalist way of life? What about American jobs? We have unemployment in this great country of ours, and he uses slave labor and exports his goods in the dead of night.

Another technique, one which can be broken into two parts: 1) Suggest Guilt by Inference and Negative Assumption, and 2) Suggest Righteousness by Positive Assumption, involves the writer's implication that the person or group being attacked is associated or related to some mutually agreed upon evil, or, as in part two, some mutually agreed upon good. The author simply ignores any evidence which would lead to conclusions other than his own. This technique appears in the parody as well as in the serious piece about abortion.

> If this bearded man is still living with his mother and likes small boys and girls, does this not fit a familiar pattern?
> In many of our churches we are warned against consorting with the Devil. The devil wears red. The Devil has pointed ears. Have you seen the pictures of Santa's helper's. Have you noticed their ears? Pointed! We are told the Devil has familiars who have strange and supernatural powers. What of Rudolph? His red nose! He flies! He sings songs in English yet! If this isn't supernatural and suspect, I don't know what is.

This second excerpt exemplifies part two of the technique.

> Twelve years ago, a ravaging cancer fell upon this country, a cancer that has taken the lives of more than 18 million children created in the image and likeness of God.

A third propaganda technique is useful when the author cannot prove to the reader that the attacked person or group is guilty of something. With Substitution of Questions for Evidence, although guilt cannot be proven, it can be implied by the way the questions are worded or by the manner in which they are asked. In this way, even the most innocent or inconspicuous act can be made to look suspect, as demonstrated by examples from the two pieces.

> Why hasn't this been presented to medical schools, let alone the public? Is it because a one-billion-dollar-a-year industry that has destroyed seventeen million pre-born children now exists in this country?

> He lives with a woman called Mrs. Claus. Nowhere in history or in the literature is there a record of their marriage or where she comes from. There are no children. Could she be his sister? Or instead of incestuous relationships, do we have to look for Oedipal possibilities? If these two are not married, what sort of role models are they?

Another common technique, Threats From Without, is successful through the author's suggestion that a danger has been imported. The reader's tribal, territorial and protective instincts are aroused and he begins to think something must be done before the threat becomes a reality. He will act much more quickly if threatened as opposed to a complacent, non-threatening situation.

The best example of this technique appears in the piece on abortion.

It was German physicians, first using mental patients, who in 1939 planned, administered, and executed the Third Reich's euthanasia program. The physicians took over the function of judge over life and death. A strong economic lever then promoted this mass violence and eight million people were slaughtered.

This technique is also employed in "The Devil's Advocate."

And what about the American capitalist way of life? Where do all of his toys come from? Not Sears. Not Penny's. Some workshop at the North Pole. Foreign imports!

The last technique is much like, Substitution of Questions for Evidence, although it does differ in one very important aspect. Pre-conclusion demand for Agreement is used to get the reader constantly responding in a positive manner and is located just before the final concluding statement, (as opposed to throughout the text as is Substitution of Questions for Evidence.) All three propaganda pieces employ this technique.

Do we really need to change the law or, do we need to restore our nation's admiration for motherhood?

Is he a terrorist or anarchist, or is he merely reacting to the worst violence in America's history—the violence that occurs daily inside the abortion clinics of America?

Is there a conspiracy of silence? Have you seen adults whispering lately? Have you heard of secret and hidden lists? Are children denied knowledge about their own futures? Are threats of reprisal more common lately? Do we have a problem?

I should say at this point that correct employment of propaganda techniques does not necessarily guarantee success, as this author discovered after attempting to create a propaganda piece. Although several of the proven effective techniques were employed, only five of the thirty persons who read "Abortion Not Wrong" were affected in the intended way. The main reason behind this partial failure is that some of the subject matter was not realistic. Although the issue addressed was a reasonable one, the situations that were proposed were rejected by most readers as being too extreme and unbelievable. However, this is not to say that the piece would not be effective on some people. Much of the effectiveness of propaganda depends upon the level at which it is written and read. Every piece of propaganda has an intended audience for which it is written. There is no piece which will successfully affect every level of readership. The five readers who did respond positively were of a much lower level readership than the other twenty-five. Even though seventeen percent of the surveyed readers did respond to the propaganda techniques, the intended readership was not affected and, therefore, the overall success was minimal.

Propaganda techniques are visible in almost all forms of communication. Propaganda material is created through a mechanical process which involves a variety of techniques that can be effective when employed correctly. Much of the effectiveness of propaganda, however, depends on the relationship between the subject matter and the intended audience. By understanding why propaganda is effective and how it works, one is capable of defending against it.

EXERCISE 12

THE DECLINE OF BUSINESS IN THE NILES AREA

A Research Paper

Presented to

Mr. Marks of the Department of English

Niles High School

by

*** ********

INTRODUCTION

   With the industrial revolution spreading across the United States like a forest fire out of control came the same kind of boom of cities which sprang up from the dust overnight around the centers of the areas that were of value to the industries. As the boom continued, a sort of alliance between the people of these towns and the industries in the towns grew and it became especially strong in the early 1900's. Among the most popular types in industries and stores were the warehouse outlet stores which carried not one type of product but a multitude of products that included every type of new and modern machinery as well as household items. These outlet stores became an important part of the industrial towns, but they became the heart of the small towns which were located far from the large cities and depended upon the outlet stores for almost every need. Two such outlet stores, Montgomery Wards and Sears and Robuck, came to the town of Niles, Michigan. Niles is located 110 miles from the nearest industrial city, Chicago, and was in need of two such outlet stores. The two stores grew quickly and became major parts of the community as well as the biggest stores in the area by the early 1900's.

   As the 1900's continued, so did the industrial revolution, but many other changes were occurring in the country at the same time that toned down the roar of the revolution. The major change was the fact that transportation was becoming more advanced and it was becoming easier for people to travel to more distant places to get their supplies. Because of this advancing transportation boom, many of the outlet stores moved out of the small town and into the larger malls where more people could go to do their shopping because they were able to get to these malls and were able to do their shopping without ever leaving the enclosed mall.

The following paper is an examination of this rapid decrease in the number of outlet stores in the small town of Niles and an in-depth look into some of the major reasons why these stores were leaving and the effect it has had on the town and its people.

Montgomery Ward was born in Niles and lived on the northeast corner of Sycamore and Front Streets.[1] At the age of seventeen, he and his family moved to St. Joseph, Michigan where he found odd jobs until he began a mail order business in Chicago Illinois.[2] His reasoning for opening such a store was based on the fact that most of the towns around the area where he was raised were small farming towns, and the people did not get in touch much with the larger cities and thus did not get as many of the modern conveniences that the people living in the cities already had. In order to bring such conveniences, such as washing machines and vacuum cleaners to the people of these small towns, he decided to build a store which would carry many different types of items, but instead of having the items in stock, he would have the people order what they wanted and the store would then get the item from another store in the city, ship it to the outlet store in the small town and thus bring the city to the people in the country.

The Montgomery Wards store in Niles opened in May of 1928 and employed approximately forty to fifty people who served about 44,000 customers from the area.[3]

---

1. Taken from the Niles Community Library's information file, news clipping of the *Niles Daily Star*, March 25, 1961.
2. Ibid.
3. Ibid., May 25, 1928

By 1933 it became the largest department store in all of southern Michigan and northern Indiana and in order to handle the growing number of people in the area, added a second floor in 1936, bringing the old store of 1,600 square feet of floor space to a total of 46,600 square feet of floor space.[4]

In August of 1950, twenty-two years after the Montgomery Wards store opened, the Sears and Robuck Company, started by Mr. Sears and Mr. Robuck for the same reason Mr. Ward started his store, opened a store in Niles to provide the same services as the Montgomery Wards store.[6] The Sears-Robuck store was located at 423 Sycamore Street and was about 19,000 square feet in size and employed about thirty-nine persons from around the Niles area. With the two outlet stores now in Niles and in full operation, Niles quickly grew in size as did the rest of the Midwest.

103

As the years passed into the 1970's however, a new type of store was coming into popularity in the United States. This was the large mall which was a huge building in which many smaller stores could rent space, thus making one building which contained not one store but many stores, all of which were inside and away from any kind of unpleasant weather. Because of this new type of store, the old outlet stores became threatened with extinction as indicated by Ward's Zone Manager, J.O. Nelson who in regards to the reasons for the closing of the Ward's facility, stated that the outlet was "Obsolete."

4. Ibid., September 30, 1953 and March 25, 1961.
5. Ibid., April 21, 1978.
6. Ibid.
7. Ibid,. April 4, 1978.

In 1979 both the Montgomery Wards and Sears-Robuck stores closed their doors and relocated their businesses at one of the two new malls in the area.[8] Two Sears officials stated, "Obviously, customers will be better served in the new University Park facility."

Shortly after the Wards and Sears-Robuck companies left Niles, several other businesses also left.[9] In regards to this sudden decline of business and the cause of the decline, Niles City Mayor Larry Clymer stated, "We're sorry to see it happen, but it does follow a national chain trend to divorce themselves from downtown areas in favor of suburban malls. The move though, combined with the loss of the other chain facilities re-establishes the fact that Niles is once again becoming a hometown community as far as downtown is concerned."[10] His statement was backed by Mr. William Clinger, Executive V.P. of the Four Flags Chamber of Commerce and a Niles citizen who said, "There's no place for the small town, green awning style store. Profits are earned in big shopping malls."[11] When asked what effect the move of the several companies in the area will have on the downtown area, Mayor Clymer responded, "The move did not sound a death blow to downtown. In the end this may strengthen us."[12]

8. Ibid., April 21, 1978.
9. Ibid.,
10. Ibid.
11. Taken from the Niles Community Library's information file, news clippings of the *South Bend Tribune*, June 11, 1978.
12. Niles Daily Star, April, 4, 1978

Montgomery Wards (1928-1979)
218 North Second Street
downtown Niles

Here was a photograph of the store building.

Sears and Robuck (1950-1979)
423 Sycamore Street
downtown Niles

Pictures taken by *** ****** on January 20, 1982.

(5)

It is really too early to tell what the true long term effects of the decline of the business in the Niles downtown area will be, but it is certain to hurt the community if the trend continues. For as fast as the industrial revolution came with all of its new ideas and machines to make life both better and easier and its effect on small towns making them grow into respectable large ones overnight, it seems it will go as equally fast, thus leaving its creations behind in the dust of its path to be written down on another page of the history books. It is very possible that Niles is becoming one of those pages. Only time will tell.

EXERCISE #13

Magazines for Everyone

America's magazine industry creates magazines which appeal to the buying public by taking under consideration the consumers' educational backgrounds, intellectual abilities, social positions, and financial conditions. Based on these factors, this country's magazine readers may be divided into three categories: low, middle, and high. A magazine is considered appropriate for a level of readership depending upon the magazine's quality and content. Therefore, it is possible, by a quick examination, to tell for whom a magazine was written. In order to identify the classification—low, middle, or high of any magazine, the cover art, table of contents, paper quality, advertisements, and letters to the editor must be studied.

Low level magazines are designed with low level readership in mind. This readership tends to have many characteristics in common, such as poor educational backgrounds, little intellectual abilities, low social positions, and poor financial conditions. Usually these magazines deal with violence, which appeals to low level readers. *Detective Cases, Master Detective, True Police, True West, True Life Secrets, True Story and True Love* are just a few low level magazines.

The colors used on the covers are bright, such as yellow, blue, red and white, in order to catch the buyers' eyes. Blurry and unrealistic photographs of lurid scenes of violence often depicting scantily clad women, are found on the covers of low level magazines. The bright colored title and blurbs, indicating the magazine's articles on violence, may be found on the front cover and hide the picture below. The following page displays the cover of the November issue of *Inside Detective* which has typical cover art characteristics, such as the bright yellow title, the white and yellow blurbs telling of a murdered child and a little boy boiled in lye, the photograph depicting violence, and the blurry and unrealistic picture. The cover's art is often a garish and poorly photographed picture depicting a scene not connected with any article in the magazine.

Displayed here was the cover of the November issue of *Inside Detective*.

A magazine's table of contents is similar to its cover in the respect that the titles are usually worded the same as the cover's blurbs. The titles are of simple wording and indicate articles about violent acts. Generally unrecognized professional writers compose many of the stories and articles in these magazines. The November issue of *Inside Detective* has a table of contents which shows typical low level characteristics, such as simply worded titles that are exactly the same as the cover's blurbs. For example, in this issue there are, "The Murdered woman in the White Jag" and "The Little Boy Was Boiled in Lye," and unknown authors such as Turke Ryder and Gary C. King. Quite often, the titles given in the tables of content suggest little of the true meaning or events of the indicated articles.

Displayed here was the table of contents of the November issue of *Inside Detective*.

The paper in low level magazines tends to be of poor quality. The soft pages are thin and have a pulpy consistency. This type of paper is not treated with waxes or plastics to cover and protect the paper and the printing. The pictures are easy to smear, and the paper does not reproduce pictures very well. The strip of paper in the right hand corner of this page is a fine example of this type of pulp paper.

Small black and white advertisements, which attempt to sell items and services such as potions of super-human strength, courses to finish high school, books on hypnosis, courses on how to become a bookkeeper, information on starting a business, x-ray glasses, aphrodisiacs, voodoo dolls, and witchcraft supplies, may be found in many low level magazines. These advertisements may be very wordy and promise much for little cost. The art work of these ads usually consist of poorly taken photographs or single line sketches. The advertisements on the following page show many of these characteristics, such as the cheap photography and inexpensive items.

Displayed here were the advertisements on page 77 of the November issue of *Inside Detective*.

Usually the letters to the editor deal with topics of the writers' personal experiences. The words *I* and *you* often are found in these letters and the writers very rarely deal with ideas. Generally the writers' vocabularies are of a limited scope and the letters contain many grammatical errors, such as run-on sentences, sentence fragments, and incorrect punctuation. These letters, as are the letters from the November issue of *Inside Detective* at the top of the page, are short and extremely unsophisticated.

The next step in magazine classification is the middle category which is designed to appeal to the middle level reader having a high school education or better, fair intellectual skills, a good social position, and a fair financial condition. Articles and stories dealing with family life, households, and health foods are commonly found in the middle level magazines. A few examples of these magazines are *Woman's Day*, *Readers' Digest*, *Red Book*, *Family Circle*, *Boys Life*, and *Weight Watchers*.

Cover art is designed to appeal to the middle level reader. Unlike low level magazines, the colors of the covers are more muted and balanced so that the covers have an equal display of bright and dark colors. The photographs and pictures are of good quality and usually depict landscapes, homes, families, housewives, and food. Fairly bright titles and some blurbs may be found on the front covers of these magazines.

The following page displays the cover of the July issue of *Family Circle* which shows the fine color qualities and color balance. The composition of an average middle level magazine is that of a well chosen picture or photograph, with all colors and shades working harmoniously together to produce a thoughtful and striking front cover.

Displayed here was the cover of the July issue of *Family Circle*.

The tables of content in middle level magazines deal with topics revealed to the reader in the blurbs on the front covers and sometimes other subjects. The titles are composed of fewer and more sophisticated words than the titles of low level magazines. Most titles correctly indicate the subject matter, such as problems of households and foods, and frequently well known writers compose stories and columns for these magazines. The following page displays the table of contents from the July issue/ of *Family circle* which shows the shorter titles, such as "The soul of America" and "Crochet Tops" by fairly known authors like Charles Kuralt and Rosemary Baskin.

Displayed here was the table of contents of the July issue of *Family Circle*.

The paper quality in these magazines tends to be of a higher quality than the pulp paper used in low level magazines. The paper is coated with waxes or plastic to protect the pages from hand oils and stains. The pages also beautifully reproduce photographs and pictures and do not smear. Some middle level magazines use both types of paper, pulp and plastic coated, such as *Readers Digest* and *Dragon*. The strip of paper in the upper right hand corner of this page is an example of the type of plastic coated paper found in middle level magazines.

Advertisements display a large variety of colorful photographs in these magazines. Usually, these ads are one to two pages long and concern topics such as food, clothes, detergents, and other household items. Like the cover art, advertisements are carefully constructed so that the colors, wording, and the products work together to display an eye-catching picture. Fewer words are used in these ads and photographs are largely used to sell the items. the following page shows an ad with typical middle level characteristics.

Displayed here was an ad for Menthol cigarettes in the July *Family Circle*.

The letters to the editors are usually written by housewives and other members of the middle level readership. These letters tend to deal with situations and experiences of others, rather than the personal experiences which are commonly found in low level magazines. The letters show a good command of the language and the fairly large vocabulary of the writers. The letters infrequently have grammatical errors and are lightly sophisticated. The following page of the July issue of *Woman's Day* shows the letters to the editor and their common characteristics, such as the good command of language and sentence structuring.

Displayed here were the letters to the editor in the May issue of *Family Circle*.

High level magazines are designed to appeal to a high level of readership, which usually has a college education, excellent intellectual ability, good financial condition, and high social position. These magazines deal with subjects of intellectual and artistic interest which include science, vacations, art, recreation, architecture and fashion. Several examples of these magazines are *Town and Country*, *Smithsonian* and *The New Yorker*.

Cover art is fashioned to attract the high level reader. The colors are very subtle and well balanced, even more so than in middle level magazines. The clear and sharp photographs and pictures are of scenes from plays, jewelry, and exotic vacation resorts. The titles are of muted colors and are often covered by the subject of the photograph or picture. Very rarely are blurbs of contents found on the covers of these magazines.

Displayed here was the cover of the August *Smithsonian*.

Tables of content in this classification of magazine deal with subjects that require high intelligence and a good education. Typically, the titles are composed of a few words and any blurbs or other information found on the covers. The cover of the August issue of *Smithsonian* is an example of the fine cover art showing the subtle colors and the high quality photography. The composition of the photographs in an average high level magazine is that of a well chosen picture or photograph with all colors working together to produce an excellent front cover.

The articles' contents are more sophisticated than those found in middle or low level magazines, All the titles correctly indicate the subject matter, such as art, vacations, and leisure. Frequently, well known professional writers write the articles of these magazines. The table of contents from the September issue of *Esquire* on the following page shows these condensed titles and more difficult wordings, such as "Unconventional Wisdom" and "Boardroom Politics at Wall Street and Vine," and the well known authors like Adam Smith and Paul Hendrickson.

Displayed here was the table of contents from the September issue of *Esquire*.

The paper quality in high level magazines is of the finest grade. Like the middle level magazines, the paper, called slick, is protected with waxes or plastics. The thick pages, similar to the example piece in the upper right hand corner on this page, reproduce photographs and pictures beautifully and do not smear.

One to two page-long advertisements of subtly colored photographs sell expensive things, such as jewelry, furs, vacation trips and luxury cars to the high level readers. These advertisements are carefully designed so that all components of the pictures, such as colors, words and the products are attractive to the readers. Few words are used in these ads and photographs are largely used to sell the items. The following page shows an ad with typical high level characteristics, such as few words and the full use of the page.

Displayed here was a full page ad for a $47,000 Rolex watch in the September issue of *The New Yorker*.

The letters to the editors are usually written by professors and other educated people. These letters tend to deal with abstract ideas rather than the personal experiences found in middle and low level magazines. The letters show an excellent command of the language and the very large vocabularies of the writers. The letters never have grammatical errors and are highly sophisticated. The following page from the August issue of *Smithsonian* shows letters and their common characteristics, such as the large vocabularies and abstract subjects.

Displayed here were the letters to the editor in the September issue of *Esquire*.

Due to the characteristics of a magazine, it is possible to determine for which readership level it was written. Therefore, since America's magazine industry designs magazines for each division of readership, every person should be able to choose a magazine which would be appropriate.

For this paper to be a really good job this student would have had to give detailed explanations of each of the examples, showing the reader how to use the examples to determine magazines' levels.

THE PROCESS
for
GETTING INTO AN EXPOSITORY PAPER

1. Before you begin expository writing, you must have an experience. This can be an assigned reading, an observation, a field trip, the examination of any material or any experience that you might have prior to writing about it.

2. Come to a conclusion about that experience. Put this conclusion into one sentence.

3. Write this sentence as a contending idea for your paper.

4. Break the explanation of the basic idea of your contention into its constituent parts.

5. Select key words to describe those parts.

6. Write the process sentence using those key words in the order in which they will introduce the material in the body of your paper.

7. Based on your reader selection, write a background. (Unless otherwise assigned, college writing is always semi-formal in tone and written for an educated adult.)

EXPOSITORY STRUCTURE

About 95% of your writing in college will be the type called expository; both argumentative and explanatory. The other few papers you will be asked to write will be your reactions to pieces you've been assigned in magazines or journals. Unless you are given instructions for the structuring of your writing assignments, the following outline will serve for your expository papers.

It might be a good idea to spend some time looking for and identifying these elements of expository papers in the student papers in this appendix.

INTRODUCTION

1. **Background** - is information that the reader will find necessary for the understanding of the contention. This can be a history of the subject or some personal experience and/or observation.

2. **Contention** - is a one-sentence statement of position or belief. This is what some teachers will call the thesis statement. This is the point of the paper and is what the body will demonstrate or prove to be true or valid. In argumentative papers, it is always assumed that the reader will not agree with your contention. If you expected your reader to agree, there would be no point in writing.

3. **Process** - is generally a one-sentence statement indicating the order in which the body parts will support the contention. As exposition is essentially statement and support; everything in the body must be related to the contention in a supportive way and must appear in the same order as indicated in the process. The key words in the breakdown of the contending idea will serve as the process (of explanation).

BODY

The **body**, which does nothing but support the contention, contains material (in as many paragraphs or sections as there are key words in the process) presented in the same order as are the points in the process. This is so that the parts of the body, each of which may be composed of a number of paragraphs, will be recognized by the reader as supporting the contending idea in the introduced order.

CONCLUSION

The **conclusion**: (has three parts, four for argumentative exposition)

1. Is a **restatement** of the contending idea but does not use the same words to describe it as you used in the introduction;

2. Is a **reintroduction** of the organizational aspects of the process but does not use the key words used in the process in the introduction;

3. Is a **connection** you make between the background, contention and body parts of your paper; and,

4. In **argumentative exposition only**, is a final statement relating to some **action or thought process** that the writer and/or the reader should go through because of the conclusions drawn from this experience.

SCHEMATIC OF AN EXPOSITORY PAPER

INTRODUCTION

1. Background
2. Contention
3. Process

BODY

The body should have as many sections as there are key words in the process.

CONCLUSION

1. Restatement of contending idea (not the same words)
2. Mention of organization (do not us same words)
3. A connection made between the body, contention and the background
4. Request for agreement (argumentative exposition only)

FORMAL	MODERATE	COLLOQUIAL
Relatively long and involved; likely to make considerable use of parallel, balanced, and periodic structures; no fragments.	Of medium length, averaging between fifteen and twenty-five words; mostly standard structure but with some parallelism and occasionally balanced and periodic sentences; fragments rare.	Short, simple structures; mainly subject-verb-object order; almost no use of balanced or periodic sentences; fragments common.

DICTION

FORMAL	MODERATE	COLLOQUIAL
Extensive vocabulary, some use of learned and abstract words; no slang, almost no contractions or clipped words.	Ranges from learned to colloquial but mostly popular words; both abstract and concrete diction; occasional contractions and clipped words; may contain some inconspicuous slang.	Diction limited to popular and colloquial words, frequent contractions and clipped words; frequent use of utility words; more slang than in moderate style.

TONE

FORMAL	MODERATE	COLLOQUIAL
Always a serious attitude toward an important subject; may be either subjective or objective and informative or affective; no attempt to establish closeness with reader, who is almost never addressed as "you"; personality of the writer not conspicuous; whole tone usually dignified and impersonal.	Attitude toward subject may be serious or light, objective or subjective, informative or affective; relationship with reader. close but seldom intimate; writer often refers to himself or herself as "I" and to reader as "you"; but the range of moderate style is so broad that it can vary from semiformal to semi-colloquial.	Attitude toward subject may be serious or light but is usually subjective; close, usually intimate, relation with reader, who is nearly always addressed as "you"; whole tone is that of informal conversation.

USES

FORMAL	MODERATE	COLLOQUIAL
A restricted style used chiefly for scholarly or technical writing for experts, or for essays and speeches that aim at eloquence or inspiration; a distinguished style, but not one for everyday use or practical affairs.	The broadest and most usable style for expository and argumentative writing and for all but the most formal of public speeches; the prevailing style in nontechnical books and magazines, in newspaper reports and editorials, in college lectures and discussions, in all student writing except some fiction.	Light, chatty writing as in letters to close friends of the same age; on the whole, a restricted style that is inappropriate to most college writing except fiction.

SAT II WRITING TEST

The writing portion of the SAT test is meant to test your knowledge of writing. It is designed to tell the testers whether you can:

1. Identify and correct mistakes in English expression,

2. Revise the writing of others, and

3. Plan and write an essay in a relatively short time.

Colleges want to know how well you do with these skills because your success in many courses in college will relate directly to your writing skills. Good grades are based not only on what you know about a subject but also on how well you can write about what you know.

The SAT II Writing Test will show your college entrance examiner how thoroughly you've mastered the skills practiced by most college writers of expository prose, the kind used for essays, reports, term papers, and other nonfiction writing—just the kind of writing skill this book was designed help you acquire.

The SAT II Writing Test consists of 60 multiple-choice questions to be answered in 40 minutes and an essay to be written in 20 minutes.

There are 30 usage questions, 18 sentence-correction questions, 12 revision-in-context questions and the written essay.

The usage questions will ask you to recognize errors in grammar and standard English usage. There will be no need to name or label the errors. You just have to find them. Nowhere on the test must you identify errors by name. ***You are not tested on your ability to tell a pronoun from a preposition.***

SAMPLE QUESTIONS

Usage Questions:

Instructions: The underlined parts of each sentence may contain an error in grammar, usage, word choice (diction), or expression. Identify the item that contains the error or choose no error.

1. The job of filling out (A) <u>several</u> job applications (B) <u>are</u> (C) <u>time-consuming</u> and (D) <u>exhausting</u>. (E) <u>No error</u>

2. Corporations (A) favor applicants with high grades, (B) varied interests and activities, and (C) they should earn (D) a good score on their application test. (E) No error

3. (A) Last week the boss announced the time of the coffee break and (B) sends all the workers a bulletin (C) that wished (D) them a good day. (E) No error

Sentence-Correction Questions:

These ask you to recognize errors in a sentence and tell which of the alternatives is the better choice. The errors may be in usage or expression or style. Your sense of what sounds best is being tested.

Instructions: The underlined sections of the sentences may contain errors in standard English. Identify which of the alternative versions best expresses the meaning of the original.
1. Many kids say that the fun they had in their junior year is greater than senior year.

   (A) than senior year
   (B) than the fun in senior year
   (C) than senior year's fun
   (D) in comparison to senior year
   (E) compared to fun in senior year.

The sample sentence compares *fun* and *senior year*, a comparison that is illogical. Since the writer meant to compare *fun* in the *junior year* with *fun* in the *senior year*, (A) cannot be right. (B) makes the comparison clear and is the right answer. (C) is grammatically correct but is weak because the phrase *fun in junior year* is not parallel to *senior year's fun*. (D) is not right because the phrase contains an awkwardly worded comparison, and (E) is wrong for the same reason.

2. Studying and taking practice tests helps students raise their grade averages.

   (A) Studying and taking practice tests
   (B) Studying and practicing tests
   (C) Studying, along with taking practice tests
   (D) By study and practicing tests
   (E) Due to studying and practicing tests

The correct answer is (C) because the sample has a compound subject. The correct verb would be *help* but you can't change *helps* to *help* because *helps* is not underlined. You must look for choices for a singular subject, one that is appropriate with the singular verb *helps*. This is (C).

3. English level has the effect _to make_ students think more about the need to write clearly.

   (A) to make
   (B) to force
   (C) in making
   (D) of making
   (E) by making

Knowing rules will not help as much here as depending on your sense of language and your ear to find the right answer. The sample sentence just doesn't feel right or sound good nor do any of the other choices except (D), which expresses the idea in ways that sound right.

Revision-in Context Questions

These questions ask you to recognize errors and weaknesses in the complete text of two students' essays. Some questions may be about grammar and usage, some about expressions and style. Most will ask you to find flaws in organization, faulty emphasis on certain ideas and illogical development or anything that characterizes poor writing.

THE ESSAY QUESTION

This is a way to see how well you write. Because you can answer questions about other's errors does not mean that you can use your language to express clearly your thinking. This essay will show college admissions officers how well you can 1) think, 2) organize ideas, 3) express those ideas, and 4) use your language.

1. You can demonstrate your ability to think by showing that you understand the topic, that you have something to say about it and that you can support your views with ideas or examples.

2. You can demonstrate your ability to organize by arranging your ideas according to a plan.

3. You can demonstrate how well you can express yourself by conveying what is in your mind to a reader. This will show that you know what you're talking about.

4. You can demonstrate your mastery of your language by using the conventions of standard written English—by writing correctly.

THE TOPIC

You will be given a general statement, and then you will be asked to agree or to disagree with the statement and to support your position with evidence taken from history, life, literature, or from your personal experience. You must not write in any other form than an essay. You should have an introduction, a body and a conclusion that are on the topic. You will be penalized for straying from the assigned topic. **This is important.**

The topics always take one of the three following forms: 1) Quotation, 2) Fill in the blank, or 3) Response to a statement, situation, or issue.

INSTRUCTIONS

Plan and write an essay in response to the assigned topic. During the 20 minutes allowed, you should develop your thoughts clearly and effectively. A plain, natural style is best. Include specific evidence or examples to support your views.

The length is up to you, but quality is more important than quantity, though one paragraph will not do. You must limit your work to the answer sheet, so use all the spaces for your work.

LENGTH

There is no required length. The College Board's readers are told to ignore the length of the essays. The development of the idea is the most important thing and not the number of words.

GRADING

Your writing will be evaluated by two readers who will read it holistically. They will spend two or three minutes and will grade it from 1 (worst) to 6 (best) based on their impression of the writing. They won't mark you down certain points for spelling or grammatical mistakes. The important thing will be your writing's cumulative effect. In this, though, everything will count some toward how the readers will feel about your work.

WRITING ASSESSMENTS AND TESTS

Universities, in their determination of who they will admit as freshmen, are now assigning major importance to the essays that are a part of every college application. They want their freshmen to be able to think and to transmit those thoughts clearly in writing. The teachers of college freshmen writing levels are despairing over the lack of skills the young people evidence. The president's report card—a report to the president of our country that is made every year about the state of education in this country—for the last 11 years has stated that over 80% of high school seniors cannot write an expository paper that makes sense. This is the kind of writing that this book is teaching you.

We have now what is called a five year liberal arts degree; so many freshmen have to take remedial English, and they get no credit for it, that it is taking them five years to finish.

Most schools are now giving what is called a holistically scored writing assessment test during freshman orientation.

The freshmen are put in a room and are given paper, pens and one-and-one-half hours to write an essay. Reproduced below are the actual directions to the teachers for scoring those essays, some directions and prompts that have been given to college freshmen and some sample essays written by them. On the basis of the scores given, the freshmen are assigned to remedial, regular, advanced English levels, or in about two percent of the cases, they are excused from taking freshmen English.

APPLICATION FORM FOR COLLEGE

Most every college application form will have directions for writing of some sort. Some will tell you to write anything that you think might help the admissions officers know you better. Some might ask you to tell about your goals in education, or your life's plans. It is **very important** that you do a good job with this section. Many applicants write just a few lines about themselves or what they feel about their education. Don't be afraid to use another page (unless the directions tell you not to), and staple it to your application. If you will be applying to a big university or a selective school, you will be in competition with lots of other bright applicants. Most will have good grade point averages, will have been in many extra-curricular activities, and will have scored well on their SAT. The thing that will make the difference will be the writing on the application.

They will be looking for that writing that is different or for original thinking. These people read thousands of applications to the big schools, and most of them are written by bright students. And most of them will sound the same. Don't be afraid to be different.

CONSIDERATIONS OF CONTENT AND STYLE
IN
MAKING WRITING ASSESSMENTS

These considerations are instructions to college teachers who are designing topics for freshmen to write on. I'm giving them to you here so you will be familiar with what your college may

119

be giving you and how it will be set up so that you might be more comfortable with it.

I CONTENT

A. **Topic**: Should seem familiar enough to promote a sense of ease in the writer and to invite expansion. The statement of the topic should provoke a feeling of competence in the writer.

The directions to make the topic familiar so the students can be expansive means that the testers will want you to give examples in your paper from your personal experience and your reading.

B. **Audience**: Should be accurately specified in terms familiar to the writer.

This means that they will either give you directions to create and specify your audience or they will direct you to write to a specific audience. This designation of audience will determine how you write your piece in terms of vocabulary, structure, tone and attitude.

C. **Choice**: should be significant or absent, and should usually be explained after both topic and audience are established.

The word choice *here refers to the second sentence you will be given. You will be given the first sentence of your paper—this will be your topic—the second sentence you will choose from two options—usually of opposite sides of some controversy. You will be expected to support your choice in the body of your paper.*

II STYLE

A. **Sentence**: Can be various in type and length in order to encourage similar varieties of usage in the writer.

It is clear that they will look for you to write in a variety of sentence styles and in different lengths.

B. **Word and Phrase**: Can be elevated or colloquial, ornamented or plain depending upon the level of language wanted from the writer.

The word and phrase choices you make must be dictated by your choice of audience. This means that you wouldn't use the same words and phrases in a letter to the president of your town's major business as you would use in a letter to the editor of your local paper or to a friend.

C. **Context and Tone**: Can be set by instructions which are authoritative but not negative in tone in order to diminish the writer's initial uncertainty, and repetitious in content in order to emphasize important requirements.

This means that they expect you to be nervous about writing and they realize that you will be under some pressure to do well, and so they will try and write your directions so as to give you encouragement and make the exercise clear. They will want you to do as well as you can.

CRITERIA FOR HOLISTIC ASSESSMENT OF A PAPER

The people who score the paper you write for your freshman orientation will be using holistic scoring techniques. The following are directions to those readers of freshmen essays in how to score them. This is valuable information for you to have, because now you will know what they will be looking for.

STRUCTURE OF WHOLE ESSAY

1. **Responds to the task** described by the instructions and accounts for the choice made.

   This means that you will want to be sure you follow the directions carefully and support the choice you make (side).

2. Maintains a **consistent point of view**:

   A. Follows through on announced purpose without shifting opinion
   B. Sustains a sense of the specified audience
   C. Sustains a uniform level of diction

   The three points they will be looking for mean that they will expect you to: 1) stick to your announced choice from the two you will be given as your second sentence; 2) write as if you were talking to the same person or people and maintain the type of word choices; and, 3) not write in one paragraph as if you were talking to your younger brother and use little words and in the next paragraph write as if you were talking to your minister.

3. Demonstrates a **clear rhetorical strategy**:

   A. Develops from beginning to end with a clear sense of introduction and conclusion

   This means that they expect you to know how to introduce ideas and wrap up a paper with concluding comments.

121

B. Integrates smoothly several levels of abstraction:

There are not many people who can do this and I don't know many teachers who would recognize if it were done well or even at all. What this means is that the readers will be looking for you to support your paper with personal experiences and/or from your reading and to meld these two types of support smoothly together so that your paper does not seem to jump from one support example to another. The word abstract *is used here in the sense of "taking part of an experience to use as support."*

C. Distinguishes between general statements, clarification, and support

This means that the evaluators of your paper will expect you to know the difference between your position, how you make your position clear and how you try to convince your reader to believe or accept your view.

D. Does not digress significantly from the central line of thought nor make lengthy repetitions of claims and/or support.

You are expected to be able to have unity in your writing—stay on track—and not repeat yourself.

SMALLER RHETORICAL AND LINGUISTIC UNITS

1. **Varies sentence structure** in a way appropriate to rhetorical purpose.

You are expected to recognize the relationship between what you say and the way you structure your sentences to say it.

2. **Understands the syntax** of the English sentence:

A. Awareness of sentence boundaries
B. Absence of errors involving misplaced parts (misplaced words, phrases and clauses, dangling modifiers), shifts in syntactic structure, and confused predication.

You are not only expected to understand what makes a sentence but also to use that understanding in your writing.

3. **Signals changes** in purpose and/or argument (*nevertheless, furthermore, on the other hand, consequently, although, etc.*) appropriately.

You are expected to tie the parts of your paper—statements and the support points—together so that the difference between these points is clear to your reader. They will be looking for the logical use of transitional devices in your writing.

122

CONVENTIONS OF STANDARD ENGLISH SURFACE FEATURES

1. **Uses** with familiarity **the conventions** of Standard English:

   A. Agreement: of subject and verb and of pronoun and antecedent
   B. Verb and tense agreement

2. **Uses** with familiarity the standard forms of **spelling, punctuation and phrasing.**

The examination lasted one hour and the directions specified the audience to whom the students were to address their essays, the purpose for which the essay was to be used, and, through sentences that students had to adopt as the beginning of their essay, the tone, level of diction, and language conventions to be used.

Each paper was read at least twice by a group of trained readers and rated of a scale of 1 to 5. Students whose essays received a score of 1 were exempted from Introductory Composition; those whose essays received a 5 were required to enroll in a special section of Introductory Composition designed for them and for which they would receive no college credit. The remaining students were required to enroll in Introductory Composition. Of the students taking this test, 2% were exempted and 7% were required to enroll in the special Introductory Composition, and 14% of all students taking the examination were judged to have serious but easily isolated problems and they were advised to obtain tutoring in writing.

ESSAY PROMPT
and
THREE STUDENT ESSAYS

The following writing prompt was given to incoming freshmen at a major university and the examples of student writing were selected as representative of four levels of production.

Write an essay which represents your position on the death penalty. Your audience is a group of your friends who, like you, will soon have the opportunity to vote for or against the abolition of the death penalty.

Begin your essay with the following sentence (which you should copy into your bluebook, a small booklet of lined paper supplied by the University):

> Prevailing penal practices often allow convicted murderers back on the streets within a short period of time.

Select one of the following as your next sentence and copy it into your bluebook:

A. Though we must denounce crime and sometimes demand more severe penalties, we must also temper justice with mercy.

B. Capital punishment, dismissed by many as a inhumane deterrent, does keep murderers from murdering again.

C. Punishment is not a humane way to treat a criminal; what is needed is an effective rehabilitation program for prisoners.

Now complete an essay which develops your position. Do your best to make your argument convincing.

The following student essays (I, II, III and IV) were written by freshmen entering college and were produced from the above writing prompt. They are reproduced here exactly as they were written. You will recognize that they are placed here in the order of writing ability.

ESSAY I

Prevailing penal practices often allow convicted murders back on the streets within a short period of time. Punishment is not a humane way to treat a criminal; what is needed is an effective rehabilitation program for prisoners. By placing a person in prison, society is making the prisoner more angry. This would account for the crimes that have been committed over and over.

There are two situations to look at when placing somebody in a prison. The first case to be looked at is whether the person actually committed the crime. All too often, innocent people are serving time for something they didn't do. If just one person has to receive this type of treatment even though he is truly innocent, that is, in itself enough reason to abolish the death penalty.

There are many ways to look at the second case also, which is somebody who actually committed the crime. Each of us has a brain, which thought processes are constantly being run through. So our minds contribute greatly to society. It's terrible to waste a human mind in life, and would be better for us all to put that thinking process to good work. Of course, the person must be able to live so as to get a chance to achieve this.

Society is way too harsh on those persons committing a crime. How do they know about each individuals background and all the problems they had. If these so-called "criminals" were accepted by society and not looked down upon, there would be less crime.

There is no way I would advocate the death penalty. People can and do change for the better. I believe those people committing crimes should be given another chance. Rehabilitation is important if done in the correct way. This way, I feel, is to let the person feel more free about himself, not trapped or encircled by guilt feelings. Rehabilitation should try to accomplish this along with putting the idea of self-worth into the prisoners mind. It may be hard to erase or over ride all the years that taught him to feel so low about himself, but with time, I feel that a sense of personal gratitude can be instilled upon him.

I truly feel that this would be the most effective method in handling prisoners, rather than prison or the death penalty. Society would benefit from having people who feel good about themselves, and the prisoner would benefit from having a new feeling and sense of accomplishment.

The reasoning being used here is that people who commit crimes have had guilt feelings most likely all their lives, especially in childhood. Having to be put down constantly is not the best type of situation to have when growing up. Parents are a major factor for inducing guilt upon a child. So why should the child have to suffer in adult life for something he couldn't prevent in the first place.

By exercising the death penalty, there is no compassion whatsoever for human feelings. Also, prison, is an everyday reminder of what you did and what you're supposed to feel bad about. No one should have to suffer for doing something which they indirectly couldn't help. All in all, the death penalty, as I see it serves no purpose whatsoever, other than wasting a good and useful human life no matter what was done or whoever may have done it.

It's easy to spot many problems with that first freshman college student's writing. Below is a much better paper.

ESSAY II

Prevailing penal practices often allow convicted murderers back on the streets within a short period of time. Though we must denounce crime and sometimes demand more severe penalties, we must also temper justice with mercy. Capital punishment cannot be used as the absolute answer to the growing crime rate in this country.

The first reason to oppose the death penalty is dependent on the jurors. Is it fair for men to decide whether or not a fellow man should lose his life for a crime he committed? Also, what

125

should happen if the jurors were wrong and the one put to death was falsely convicted; death is irreversible.

The second problem with the death penalty is its connotations as a punishment. Is the government actually condoning murder by committing them themselves? It seems like the death penalty is a step backward for Americans, killing men for murders occurring while a certain law is in effect.

It is still possible to find many things wrong with this writer's ability, but it is a much better paper.

ESSAY III

Prevailing penal practices often allow convicted murders back on the streets within a short period of time. Though we must denounce crime and some times demand more severe penalties, we must temper justice with mercy.

It is becoming increasingly obvious that the American penal system needs to be changed. Prisons are overcrowded, the courts are backed up, and while some criminal offenders are being mistreated and dehumanized by the system, others are being set free through parole and early release programs which often create a danger to the public. There can be no quick and easy solution to these problems, but there are several factors that, when examined, can help create an understanding of the causes.

The first is the fact that rehabilitation, when available, is offered only after an offense has been committed. At this point it is usually too late to help the criminal change his way of life. Instead, therapy and other professional help services should be offered at the adolescent and young-adult level, before the criminal lifestyle develops. Even elementary schools should have some method to help children with criminal tendencies. These services should be free and available to all.

Another problem creating factor is that the technicalities of the law can keep serious offenders on the streets. No matter how obvious the guilt of a defendant is, a forgotten question or illegal search can get him a dismissal and complete freedom. Laws such as these must be restructured to ensure the safety of the people and the effectiveness of the judicial system.

There are many other factors which have contributed to the downfall of the American penal system. Unless analyzed and the problems solved, a complete breakdown of justice as we know it may occur.

Prevailing penal practices often allow convicted murderers back on the street within a short period of time. Punishment is not a humane way to treat a criminal; what is needed is an effective rehabilitation program for prisoners. If we are to do anything to stop the increasing rate of crime, we must begin from the source: the attitudes of the criminals themselves.

One of the main drawbacks of the present penal system is its main tool used against criminals: incarceration. The current prisons have nothing to offer criminals except a place of confinement, which helps to build resentment and offers the opportunity for the inmate to plan more crimes. Evidence of this is in the current recidivism rate: it has been estimated that close to 90% of all crimes are committed by repeat offenders.

Having realized that incarceration does not stop crime, but actually breed it, people have tried to determine other ways to handle criminals. Perhaps the most newsworthy, and therefore the most controversial, is the death penalty. Backers of the death penalty feel it is the only way to bring down the murders and slow down the increasing crime rate. But even by saying so, they are admitting defeat. They are telling us that society has failed in its effort to control an individual, and so society is therefore ridding itself of that individual. Claiming that the death penalty is necessary is admitting that society, with all its psychiatrists, social workers, and special organizations and departments, has gone down to defeat to one individual. The answer, then is to destroy the competition.

But this is not the way of the society we live in. We have the necessary tools; all we need to do is to put them to use. One of our most important assets is our people. We have the people with the determination and the patience to work with these criminals, to help them get back in with the rest of society. These people won't admit defeat, but keep on trying until the job is done.

What is required, then, is to shift the attitude of and the basis for today's penal system. Its purpose must become rehabilitation, not incarceration and punishment.

We can start right in the prisons. Many ideas have been successfully tried at rehabilitation centers and certain prisons; ideas such as community employment. The inmate is allowed to go to a regular job during the day, but return to the center or prison after the job. Sessions are held with each inmate, as well as group sessions for all who are participating in the program. The idea is to get the inmate ready to return to society, partly by making him feel he is contributing something to society. It is a complete switch from the practice of simply letting a prisoner go out the door after his term is up, and it works. One state working with these rehabilitation centers found that nearly 95% of those inmates who participated in the program before leaving prison have not committed a crime since.

Our goal must be to make former inmates into members of society, rather than ridding ourselves of them. This can only be accomplished by making them a useful part of society, something that they're not when they're sitting in a cell. We will then have won a victory for society that we will all benefit from, rather than admitting defeat.

If you have to take such a test, you can expect to have prompts similar to the following, which have been used in major universities:

First sentence:

By the time the average person in North America graduates from high school, she or he will have seen 18,000 hours of television.

Second sentence choices:

1. *The present generation of preschoolers watches an average of 54 hours of television each week.*

2. *Dr. Edward Palmer, head of research at Sesame Street writes: "I think that watching television is a rather remarkable act in itself. All the while kids are watching, they're actively relating what they're seeing to their own lives."*

3. *Since real experience is the primary source of learning, our children are growing up addicted to television and ignorant of life.*

And yet another prompt. It would pay you to practice writing essays demanded by prompts such as these.

First sentence:

The need of and the ability to pay for an education for everyone has changed in the last 20 years.

Two choices for your second sentence:

> *1.   Compulsory education is no longer necessary.*
>
> *2.   Compulsory education is more essential now than ever before.*

It is possible that you will be given writing directions and a prompt similar to this:

> *You are to write a brief (200-400 words) but complete essay concerning one of the topics listed below. The style and form of your essay should be appropriate for writing in college-level course work. Because of the limited time available, you obviously will not be able to produce a perfectly finished paper, rather, you should attempt to write as good a first draft as possible, crossing out words or sentences if necessary, and leaving a few minutes to proofread and revise your work. Although it is important to spend some time planning your essay, it is also important to get started writing as quickly as possible.*
>
> *1. If you could spend a year in any country other than the United States, what country would you choose? Support your choice with as many reasons as possible.*
>
> *2. You are a member of the age group which most television advertisers view as their prime target—you are the persons to whom they are trying to sell shampoo, toothpaste, beer, cars, deodorants and mouthwashes, etc. Is their money well spent? In composing your essay you should keep the following questions in mind: How attractive is current commercial TV programming to America's young adults? How influential are the commercials that support the programming?*
>
> *3. Starting January 1, in some states, smoking in government buildings and public places such as auditoriums, arenas and museums will be prohibited. Consider the advantages and disadvantages of your state passing this limitation. How would you vote if you were a legislator? Why?*

Here is a writing prompt used at a university that gives a specific audience for the freshmen to write to.

> *Write an essay intended to help a Senate sub-committee on technology consider how computers influence the quality of human life.*
>
> *Begin your essay with the following sentence:*

While increasing the flow of money, goods, and information, computers are changing human interaction by decreasing direct contact between people.

Select one of the following as your second sentence:

1. *Although this is true, computerizing data is a necessary response to our society's complex needs.*

2. *For many areas such as law and medicine, this decreased contact is compensated for by increased speed and accuracy.*

3. *When people become more distant from each other, individual differences are less understood and therefore less valued.*

You will be required to take examinations in most of your courses, and many of them will be of the essay type. You can save yourself trouble by studying and even practicing with the following material.

POINTERS ON TAKING AN ESSAY EXAMINATION

I. **Studying for an Essay Exam**: (Important)

  A. Always take good notes and review them.
  B. Think about your facts and understand them.
    1. Recognize relationships between points and think of supporting arguments.
      a) Points that are similar
      b) Points that are different
    2. Ask yourself questions—such as:
      a) Why something happened; or,
      b) How it happened etc.
    3. You have to know what you're talking about because you can't fake it on an essay test.

II. **Before Starting the Exam**:

  A. Look over questions quickly
    1. See how many there are.
    2. See how much time you'll have. Some tests have time limits on each question, therefore, it will be expected that the question with the longer allowed time will have more work done on it, because it will most likely deal with important or complex issues relating to the course.

III. **Think Before Writing**:

  A. Know exactly what is being asked.
    1. Pay attention to punctuation because it can change the meaning of a question.
    2. Mark important words in the question to keep you on the right track.

IV. **Hints for Answering Questions**:

  A. Organize your thoughts by making a quick outline.
  B. Narrow Questions:
    1. Quotations give you clues to what your grader wants you to talk about.
      a) Never attack the author of a quote.
      b) You can attack the quote if you don't agree with it.
  C. Broad Questions:
    1. Again, look for hints in the question.
    2. Two most used words in essay exams:
      a) *Compare*—showing in what ways two or more words are alike.
      b) *Contrast*—showing in what ways two or more things differ.

V. **Beginning Your Answer**: (introduction)
   A. **The Do's**:
      1. The best way to start is to directly begin answering the question.
      2. List the facts you are going to write about in the first sentence and then go on to write about them.

   B. **The Do not's**:
      1. Never repeat the question.
      2. Don't give facts that don't deal with the question. (You only waste time.)
      3. Don't try to be funny by making jokes.

VI. **Body**

   A. Essay answers are basically arguments and you can either **attack** or **defend** the position taken in the question. You should use:
      1. Logic—exact reasoning and argumentation,
      2. Evidence—presented to make the argument clear and believable,
      3. Relevance—the information necessary for an effective answer,
      4. Simple order of presentation is best—some students feel that to give really involved answers makes them look smarter and that simplicity is a mark of ignorance, but this isn't true,
         a) Chronological order if possible
         b) Analysis
            1) Deduction—each step is based on preceding proven or known statements until the problem is solved
            2) Induction—(opp. of deduction) Proving a guess by using facts, events or processes
            3) Analogy—showing that things, processes or events are alike (comparative)

VII. **Concluding—The Answer**:

   A. **Do's**:
      1. If there is time, summarize the main points of the answer. (Teachers like this.)
      2. If there is not time, finish with the "More could be said" device. Give a list of other data or sources, but this only works if it relates to your answer.
      3. If you are in a hurry: Use the major terms of the question, such as: "These are the most important ways that. . ."

   B. **Do not's**:
      1. No apologies
      2. No excuses—"Not enough time"
      3. No punch lines

COMMON WRITING PROBLEMS
and
HOW TO AVOID THEM

AMBIGUITY

A statement may be taken in two ways.

1. She saw the man walking down the street.

   This can mean either:
   A. *She saw the man when **she** was walking down the street; or,*
   B. *She saw the man when **he** was walking down the street.*

2. The use of pronouns *it, she, they, them* that do not have clear antecedents (what they refer to) can create ambiguous sentences:

   Bill looked at the coach when <u>he</u> got the money.

   This can mean either:
   A. *When Bill got the money **he** looked at the coach; or,*
   B. *Bill looked at him when **the coach** got the money.*

APOSTROPHE

An apostrophe (') is a mark used to indicate possession or contraction.

Rules:

1. To form the possessive case (who owns it) of a singular noun (one person or thing), add an apostrophe and an *s*.

   Example: *the girl's coat   Bill's ball   the car's tire*

2. To form the possessive case of a plural noun (two or more people or things) ending in *s*, add only the apostrophe.

   Example: *the boys' car   the cars' headlights*

3. Do not use an apostrophe for: *his, hers, its, ours, yours, theirs, whose.*

   Example: *The car was theirs.   The school must teach its students.*

4. Indefinite pronouns: (could be anyone) *one, everyone, everybody,* require an apostrophe and an *s* to show possession.

   Example: *One's* car is important.   That must be *somebody's* bat.

5. An apostrophe shows where letters have been omitted in a contraction (making one word out of two).

   Example: *can't* for cannot   *don't* for do not
            we've for we have   *doesn't* for does not

   Note that the apostrophe goes in the word where the letter or letters have been left out.

6. Use an apostrophe and an *s* to make the plural of letters, numbers and of words referred to as words.

   Example: There are three *b's* and two *m's* in that sentence.
            It was good back in the *1970's.*
            Do not say so many "*and so's*" when you explain things.

AUDIENCE

Writers don't just write. They write to selected readers in specific forms for purposes. To be effective, writers must decide what form is most appropriate for their intended readers so that they can accomplish their purposes.

Keep in mind that, just as you talk differently to different audiences, you must write differently also. You wouldn't talk to your mother or your minister the same way you'd talk to friends.

As you read your writing, think of who your intended audiences are and try and judge how what you're saying will influence those people.

Examples:

1. Informal—colloquial: (used with friends in friendly letters and notes):

   Man, that was a such a dumb test, I just flunked it.

2. Semiformal: (used in themes, tests, and term papers in school and in letters and articles to businesses and newspapers):

   The test was very hard and so I did not do well.

3. Formal: (seldom used by students but appropriate for the most formal of written communication on the highest levels of government, business or education):

   The six-week's examination was of sufficient scope to challenge the knowledge of the best of the students in the class. Not being adequately prepared for it, I did not demonstrate my true ability.

AWKWARD WRITING

Awkward writing is rough and clumsy. It can be confusing to the reader and make the meaning unclear. Many times just the changing of the placement of a word or the changing of a word will clear up the awkwardness.

If you read your work out loud or have someone read it to you and then to listen to what they're saying, you can catch the awkwardness. Remember that you have to read loud enough to hear your own voice.

1. *Each of you kids will have to bring each day each of the following things: pen, pencil and paper.*

   This should be rewritten to read:

   Each day bring pens, pencils and paper.

2. *The bird flew down near the ground, and having done this, began looking for bugs or worms, because it was easier to see them down low than it had been when it was flying high in the sky.*

   There are many problems with that sentence. To get rid of its awkwardness, it could be rewritten to read:

   The bird, looking for food, swooped low.

135

Keep in mind that the point of your writing is for them to give your readers information. The simplest way to do this may be the best way.

CLICHÉ

All young writers like to use expressions they've heard or read. It makes them feel that they're writing like adult authors. Many times you'll use expressions that you didn't realize have been used so many times before that they no longer are fresh and exciting for their readers:

round as a dollar   *pretty as a picture*   *tall as a tree*   *snapped back to reality*
stopped in his tracks *stone cold dead*   *fell flat on his face* *roared like a lion*
white as a sheet   *graceful as a swan*   *stiff as a board*   *limber as a willow*

Usually the first expressions young writers think of when they write will be clichés. If you think you've heard of an expression before, don't use it, but think of ways to tell your readers what you want them to know using expressions that are new.

COMMAS

I am including commas because they are often seen as such a problem. Young people cannot learn all of the comma rules at once. Some will never learn them all. All writers have some comma placement rules they ignore. One thing that will help you is to read your work out loud and to listen to where your voices drop inside sentences. That is where a comma goes. This will work for about 95% of comma placement. This works because commas are needed and used to make clear the meaning in writing. They indicate a pause or a separation of ideas.

Rules: You should use commas in the following situations:

1. To separate place names—as in an address, dates, or items in a series
2. To set off introductory or concluding expressions
3. To make clear the parts of a compound sentence
4. To set off transitional or non-restrictive words or expressions in a sentence

Examples:

1. *During the day on May 3, 1989, I began to study.*

   I had courses in English, math and geography at a little school in Ann Arbor, Michigan.

The parts of the date should be separated by commas, and the courses in this sentence which come in a list should be separated by commas. Your have a choice of whether to put a comma before the *and* just prior to the last item on a list.

2. *After the bad showing on the test, Bill felt he had to study more than he had.*

    The introduction—*After the bad showing on the test*—to the central idea of this sentence—*Bill felt he had to study more*—is set off from this central idea by a comma.

3. *Bill went to class to study for the test, and I went to the snack bar to feed the inner beast.*

    There are two complete ideas here: 1) *Bill went to study*; and, 2) *I went to eat*. These two ideas can be joined in a compound (two or more things put together) sentence if there is a conjunction *(and, but, though)* between them and they are separated by a comma. Notice where the comma is placed in the example below.

4. *Bob, who didn't really care, made only five points on the test.*

    The idea of this fourth sentence is that Bob made only five points on the test. The information given that he didn't care is interesting but not essential to the understanding of the main idea of the sentence. The commas indicate that the words between them are not essential to the meaning of the sentence.

COMMA SPLICE

A comma splice is when the two halves of a compound sentence are joined/separated by a comma.

Example: *Bill had to take the test over again, he felt sorry he would miss the party.*

A comma splice can be avoided by writing this sentence in one of the five following ways:

1. *Bill had to take the test over again and felt sorry he would miss the party.*

2. *Bill had to take the test over again; he felt sorry he would miss the party.*

3. *Bill had to take the test over again, and he felt sorry he would miss the party.*

4. *Bill had to take the test over again: he felt sorry he would miss the party.*

5. *Bill had to take the test over again. He felt sorry he would miss the party.*

Notice that the punctuation of each of the above examples gives the reader a different idea about Bill and how he felt.

DIALOGUE STRUCTURE and PUNCTUATION

Dialogue is conversation between two or more people. When shown in writing, it refers to the speech or thoughts of characters.

Rules: Dialogue can occur either in the body of the writing or on a separate line for each new speaker.

Examples:

1.   *John took his test paper from the teacher and said to him, "This looks like we'll get to know each other well." The teacher looked surprised and said with a smile, "I hope so."*

2.   *John took his test paper from the teacher and said to him, "This looks like you and I'll get to know each other well."*
       The teacher looked surprised and said with a smile, "I hope so."

3.   *John took his test paper from the teacher and thought, "This looks like I'll get to know this old man well this year." The teacher looked surprised—almost as if he had read John's mind—and thought, "I hope so."*

DICTION

Diction is the words chosen—your vocabulary as you use it.

Rules: There are at least four levels of diction:
1. FORMAL: The words of educated people when they are being serious with each
                    other.

   Example: *Our most recent suggestion was the compromise we felt we could make under the present circumstances.*

2. INFORMAL: Polite conversation of people who are relaxed.

   Example: *We have given you the best offer we could.*

3. COLLOQUIAL: Everyday speech by average people.

   Example: *That was the best we could do.*

4. SLANG: Ways of talking that are never used in writing except in dialogue to show characterization.

 Example: *It's up to you, cook or get outa the kitchen.*

FLOWERY WRITING

You'll use flowery writing when you want to impress your readers with how many good words you can use to express ideas. This results in the words used becoming more important than the ideas presented.

Rule: A general rule that should apply is: What you say should be put as simply as possible.

 Example: *The red and fiery sun slowly settled into the distant hills like some great, billowing sailing ship sinking beyond the horizon. It cast its pink and violet flags along the tops of the clouds where they waved briefly before this ship of light slid beneath the waves of darkness and cast us all, there on the beach, into night.*

 This is so flowery that it is hard to read without laughing. It should be rewritten to read:

 We remained on the beach gazing at the darkening sky while the sun set.

MODIFIER (dangling)

This means that there is nothing for the modifier to modify in the sentence.

 Examples: *Getting up, my arms felt tired.* (How did the arms get up all by themselves?)

 This should read: *When I got up my arms felt tired.*

 Coming down the street, my feet wanted to turn into the park. (Again, how did the feet do this?)

 This should read: *Coming down the street, I felt as if my feet wanted to turn toward the park.*

 Being almost asleep, the accident made me jump. (It is clear the accident could not have been asleep.)

 This should read: *I was almost asleep and the accident made me jump.*

PARAGRAPH

A paragraph is a sentence or a group of sentences developing one idea or topic.

Rules: In nonfiction writing, a paragraph consists of a topic sentence which is supported by other sentences giving additional details. A good rule is: A paragraph in this kind of writing should have at least four supportive sentences, making at least five sentences for every paragraph.

Example:

TOPIC SENTENCE: One sentence that introduces the reader to the main idea of the paragraph.

PARAGRAPH DEVELOPMENT: May be made by facts, examples, incidents, comparison, contrast, definition, reasons (in the form of arguments) or by a combination of methods.

PARALLELISM

Parallelism is two or more parts of a single sentence, having equal importance—being structured the same way.

Examples:

1. *We went home to eat and reading.* This should read: *We went home to eat and to read.* This is obvious in such a short sentence, but this is an easy mistake to make when the sentences get complicated.

2. *There are a number of things that a boy must think about when he is planning to take a bike trip. He must think about checking the air pressure in his tires, putting oil on the chain, making sure the batteries in his light are fresh and to make sure his brakes work properly.*

Notice that in this list there is a combination of four parallel participles and one infinitive which cannot be parallel in structure. (This sounds like English-teacher talk.)

What it means is the first three items on the list: (1) *checking,* (2) *putting* (3) *making* are parallel, but the fourth item on the list, (4) *to make,* is not structured the same way, and so this last item is not parallel in structure with the first three items. This sentence should be rewritten to read: *He must think about checking the air pressure in his tires, putting oil on the chain, making sure the batteries in his light are fresh and making sure his brakes work properly.*

PRONOUN REFERENCE and AGREEMENT

To keep writing from being boring, pronouns are often used instead of nouns.

Rules: It must be clear to the reader which noun the pronoun is replacing. The pronoun must agree in case, gender and number with that noun. The most common error young writers make is with number agreement.

Examples:

Betty and Janet went to the show, but she didn't think it was so good. (It's not clear which girl didn't like the show.)

If a child comes to dinner without clean hands, they must go back to the sink and wash over. (The word *they* refers to "a child" and the number is mixed. This should read: *If children come to dinner without clean hands they should go back. . .)*

Both boys took exams but Bob got a higher score on it. (The pronoun *it* refers to the noun *exams* and the number is mixed here.)

Everybody should go to the show, and they should have their tickets handy. (The problem here is that the word *everybody* is singular and the pronouns *they* and *their* are plural.) The following words are singular and they need singular verbs: *everybody, anybody, each, someone.*

QUOTATION MARKS

Quotation marks are used to indicate exact words or thoughts and to indicate short works and chapters of long works.

Rule: 1. You should put in quotation marks the direct quotation of a person's words. When you use other marks of punctuation with quotation marks: 1) you should put commas and periods inside the quotation marks; and, 2) put other punctuation marks inside the quotation marks if they are part of the quotation; if they are not part of the quotation, you should put them outside of the quotation marks.

Example: *The salesman said, "This is the gum all the kids are chewing."*

Rule: 2. Put in quotation marks the titles of chapters, articles, other parts of books or magazines, short poems, short stories and songs.

Example: *In this magazine there were two things I really liked: "The Wind Blows Free" and "Flowers," the poems by the young girl.*

REDUNDANCY

Redundancy means using different words to say the same thing. The writer doesn't gain by this, only confuses and bores the reader.

Examples: *I, myself, feel it is true.*
It is plain and clear to see.
Today, in the world, there is not room for lack of care for the ecology.

This is an easy mistake to make, and it will take conscious thought for you to avoid this problem. You'll have to have help to find redundancies in your work. There are no exercises you can do which will help; just use care when you're proofreading your work.

SENTENCE

RUN-ON: This is the combining of two or more sentences as if they were one.

Example: *Bill saw that the fish was too small he put it back in the lake and then put a fresh worm on his hook.* (This sentence needs to be broken into two sentences by putting a period between small and he. It could also be correct with a semicolon between small and he.)

FRAGMENT: This is part of a sentence which lacks a subject or a verb or both.

Check your sentences to make sure they have both subjects and verbs.

Some writers use fragments effectively. You may do this in your creative writing. You should avoid using fragments in expository papers.

Examples: Fragments can be powerful if used correctly:

When Janet reached her door she found it was partly open. A burglar! Someone had been in her house and had left the door open.

SENTENCE VARIETY

Young writers have a tendency to structure all or most of their sentences in the same way.

Give variety to the structuring of your sentences. A common problem for young writers is that of beginning most sentences with a subject-verb pattern.

Examples: *Janet bought a car. The car was blue. It had a good radio. She liked her car and spent a lot of time in it.*

These sentences could be re-written and combined so they all do not start with a subject and verb.

> *The car Janet bought was blue. Because she liked it so much, she spent a lot of time in it.*

SUBJECT-VERB AGREEMENT (number)

Closely related words have matching forms, and, when the forms match, they agree. Subjects and their verbs agree if they both are singular or both are plural.

Rules: Singular subjects require singular verbs, and plural subjects require plural verbs.

Singular: *car, man, that, she, he, it*

Plural: *cars, men, those, women, they*

Singular: *The heater was good.   The heater works well.*

Plural: *The heaters were good.   The heaters work well.*

Most nouns form their plural by adding the letter *s*, as in *bats* and *cats*. The clue is the final *s*.

It is just the opposite with most verbs. A verb ending in *s* is usually singular, as in *puts, yells, is* and *was*.

Most verbs not ending in *s* are plural, as in *they put, they yell*. The exceptions are verbs used with *I* and singular *you*: *I put, you put*.

Problems come when there is a phrase or clause between the subject and verb.

Example: *This red car, which is just one of a whole lot full of cars, is owned by John and Bob.* (It is easy for some young writers to think that cars is the plural subject and write the sentence this way: *This red car, which is just one of a whole lot full of cars, are owned by John and Bob.* The subject of this sentence *This red car* is singular; there are just a lot of words between the subject and the verb, and it confuses the number.)

TENSE ERROR

Tense errors occur when past and present tenses are mixed and there is no justification for changing.

Rules:

1. Present tense is used to describe actions that are taking place at the time of the telling of the event.

   Example: *John is in the house. Mr. Jones lives there.*

2. Past tense is used to describe actions that have already happened.

   Example: *John was in the house. Mr. Jones lived there.*

3. Future tense is used to describe actions that will happen.

   Example: *John will be in the house. Mr. Jones will live there.*

TRANSITIONS

Transitions are bridges from one idea to the next or from one reference to the next or from one section of a paper to the next.

Rule: It will help your readers if you aid them in their reading by bridging their ideas for them. This can be done by:

1. Using linking words like: *however, moreover, thus,* and *because* and phrases like: *on the other hand, in effect,* and *as an example.*

2. Repeating words and phrases used earlier in the writing.

3. Referring to points used previously.

   Examples: If you were to write two paragraphs about pets—a cat and a dog, it would be necessary for you to make some transition between the two paragraphs—the one about the cat and the one about the dog.

Below is the ending of a paragraph about a cat and the beginning of a paragraph about a dog. The idea of having fun with the cat will serve as a transition to the paragraph about having fun with the dog.

> *. . .and so I get a great deal of pleasure from my cat. She and I have a lot of fun together.*
> *My dog, on the other hand, gives me pleasure and fun of a different nature. We spend time. . .*

144

VOICE   (passive and active)

Most sentences are built on the order of subject-verb-object. This produces an active voice. If a passive verb is used, it inverts this order and makes it seem as if the object were doing rather than receiving the action of the verb.

Your writing will be more forceful if you use an active voice.

Examples:

Active: *Bill threw the ball.   We must spend this money.   Bill drove the car with care.*

Passive: *The ball was thrown by Bill.   This money must be spent by us. The car was driven with care by Bill.*

Rule: You can use a passive voice if:

1. The doer of the action is unknown

2. The action needs to be emphasized

3. The receiver of the action is of more importance than the doer of the action.

Examples:
1. *When we were gone, the house was burglarized.*   (The one who broke in is unknown.)

2. *No matter how hard they played, the game was lost.* (The game being lost is the most important thing.)

3. *My pet mouse was eaten by that cat.* (The mouse is more important than the cat.)

WRONG WORD

The words you use do not always mean what you think they do.

Rule:
You should not try and use words in your writing that you don't feel comfortable with while talking. If you would never say the words *alas* or *to no avail* or *travail,* you should not write them.

National Writing Institute Order Form

		Qty.	Total
☐	***Writing Strands* Level 1** Oral work for ages 3-8 $14.95 ea.	___	___
☐	***Writing Strands* Level 2** About 7 years old $18.95 ea.	___	___
☐	***Writing Strands* Level 3** Starting program ages 8-12 $18.95 ea.	___	___
☐	***Writing Strands* Level 4** Any age after Level 3 or starting program at age 13 or 14 $18.95 ea.	___	___
☐	***Writing Strands* Level 5** Any age after Level 4 or starting program at age 15 or 16 $20.95 ea.	___	___
☐	***Writing Strands* Level 6** 17 or any age after Level 5 $20.95 ea.	___	___
☐	***Writing Strands* Level 7** 18 or any age after Level 6 $22.95 ea.	___	___
☐	***Writing Exposition*** Senior high school and after Level 7 $22.95 ea.	___	___
☐	***Creating Fiction*** Senior high school and after Level 7 $22.95 ea.	___	___
☐	***Evaluating Writing*** Parents' manual for all levels of *Writing Strands* $19.95 ea.	___	___
☐	***Reading Strands*** Parents' manual for story and book interpretation, all grades $22.95 ea.	___	___
☐	***Communication and Interpersonal Relationships*** Communication manners (teens) $17.95 ea.	___	___
☐	***Dragonslaying Is for Dreamers* - package** 1st novel in *Dragonslaying* trilogy (early teens) and parents' manual for analyzing the novel. $18.95 ea.	___	___
☐	***Dragonslaying Is for Dreamers* - novel only** $9.95 ea.	___	___
☐	***Axel Meets the Blue Men*** 2nd novel in *Dragonslaying* trilogy (teens) $9.95 ea.	___	___
☐	***Axel's Challenge*** Final novel in *Dragonslaying* trilogy(teens) $9.95 ea.	___	___
☐	***Dragonslaying* trilogy** All three novels in series $25.00 set	___	___

SUBTOTAL: ___
Texas residents add **7.75%** sales tax ___
U.S. Shipping:
$2.00 per book (**$4.00 Minimum**).................... ___

Outside U.S. Shipping:
$4.00 per book (**$8.00 Minimum**).................... ___

TOTAL U.S. FUNDS:
☐ CHECK or MONEY ORDER........................... ___
☐ CREDIT CARD.. ___

☐ VISA ☐ DISCOVER ☐ MasterCard

Account Number

☐☐☐☐ - ☐☐☐☐ - ☐☐☐☐ - ☐☐☐☐

Expiration date: Month ☐☐   Year ☐☐

_____
Signature

(PLEASE PRINT) We ship U.P.S. to the 48 states, so please no P.O. #.

Name: _____

Street: _____

City: _____

State: _____ Zip: _____

Phone: (_____) _____

E-Mail (if available) _____

SHIPPING INFORMATION

Continental US : We ship via UPS ground service. Most customers will receive their orders within 10 business days.

Alaska, Hawaii, US Military addresses and US territories: We ship via US Priority Mail. Orders generally arrive within 2 weeks.

Canada: We ship via Air Mail. Most customers receive orders within 2 weeks.

Other international destinations: We generally ship via Air Mail. Delivery times vary.

RETURNS

Our books are guaranteed to please you. If they do not, return them within 30 days and we'll refund the full purchase price.

PRIVACY

We respect your privacy. We will not sell, rent or trade your personal information.

INQUIRIES AND ORDERS:

Phone:	(800) 688-5375 TOLLFREE
Fax:	(888) 663-7855 TOLLFREE
Write:	**National Writing Institute** 624 W. University #248 Denton, TX 76201-1889
E-mail:	info@writingstrands.com
Website:	www.writingstrands.com

NEW ADDRESS